MILITARY THEORY AND
THE CONDUCT OF WAR

AZAR GAT

Military Theory and the Conduct of War

What Is Strategy All About?

OXFORD
UNIVERSITY PRESS

Oxford University Press is a department of the
University of Oxford. It furthers the University's objective
of excellence in research, scholarship, and education
by publishing worldwide.

Oxford New York
Auckland   Cape Town   Dar es Salaam   Hong Kong   Karachi
Kuala Lumpur   Madrid   Melbourne   Mexico City   Nairobi
New Delhi   Shanghai   Taipei   Toronto

With offices in
Argentina   Austria   Brazil   Chile   Czech Republic   France   Greece
Guatemala   Hungary   Italy   Japan   Poland   Portugal   Singapore
South Korea   Switzerland   Thailand   Turkey   Ukraine   Vietnam

Oxford is a registered trade mark of Oxford University Press
in the UK and certain other countries.

Published in the United States of America by
Oxford University Press
198 Madison Avenue, New York, NY 10016

Copyright © Azar Gat, 2025

All rights reserved. No part of this publication may be reproduced,
stored in a retrieval system, or transmitted, in any form or by any means,
without the prior permission in writing of Oxford University Press,
or as expressly permitted by law, by license, or under terms agreed with
the appropriate reproduction rights organization. Inquiries concerning
reproduction outside the scope of the above should be sent to the
Rights Department, Oxford University Press, at the address above.

You must not circulate this work in any other form
and you must impose this same condition on any acquirer.
Library of Congress Cataloging-in-Publication Data is available

ISBN: 9780197828489

Printed in the United Kingdom
by Bell & Bain Ltd, Glasgow

Contents

Introduction: The Quest for a General Theory
for the Conduct of War   1

1. The Nature of War: What Can Be Derived from
   It for the Conduct of Military Operations?   17
   Political Objectives and Military Means—
      Yet Another Look   17
   What Is Victory in War?   22
   War as Adversarial and Violent—
      and the Rationale of Military Operations   28
   Defense and Attack: Is the Defense the Stronger
      Form; or Is Offense the Best Defense?   34
   How to Determine What Is in the 'Nature of War'—
      and What Is Historically Shaped and Transitory?   42

2. History and Military Doctrine   49
   The 'Levels' of the Conduct of War   51
   Enter the Concept of Doctrine:
      Military Revolutions—Past and Present   54
   How Has Guerrilla Become a Recipe for Success?   67

	Terrorism: Eternal or New? And Where Is It Heading?	84
	The Ultimate Weapon	95
3.	War—Now and Forever?	103
	The Nature of War and Human Nature: Is War Inevitable?	103
	Is War Declining—Why and Where?	109

Conclusion	133
Notes	145
Index	159

INTRODUCTION
THE QUEST FOR A GENERAL THEORY FOR THE CONDUCT OF WAR

The question of how we should think about the theory of war and its conduct—and whether there is something that can be regarded as a general, universal theory in this field—has long preoccupied military personnel, scholars, and other students of military affairs. Yet it has rarely been the subject of direct investigation. War and its conduct have changed across history, most notably under the influence of successive technological revolutions during modern times. But is there anything enduring about them that can be determined, taught as such in professional settings, and applied in practice? Some have employed a distinction between the 'face' or 'character' of war, which is changing, and its 'nature', which is supposedly (more or less) fixed. But what is this 'nature'?

The problem of continuity versus change first presented itself during the eighteenth-century Enlightenment and has remained with us ever since.[1] The question had scarcely troubled people before. During premodern times, the prevailing, classical view was that the world and human reality were basically unchanging. The slow and limited historical change—economic, social, political, technological, and military—that people were able to observe during the time span in historical memory with which they were familiar was not noticeable enough to shake this view. Thus, the classical precepts on politics and social affairs, expressing the features of quite a static agrarian society, were regarded as being of lasting applicability. In classical Greece, if not in the great autocratic civilizations of Asia, socio-political thought was even able to catalogue three regime types familiar from the Greek political landscape—autocracy, aristocracy, and democracy—which were believed to rotate and replace one another in a never-ending cycle.

That same static picture of human reality applied to the military field as well. Works by classical military authors such as Xenophon, Polybius, Caesar, Arrian, Vegetius, Frontinus, Aelian, Polyaen, Vitruvius, and the Byzantine emperors Maurice and Leo, who essentially summarized the military practices of their times, were regarded as possessing general applicability and hence lasting value, long after they were written. Very little fundamental change from their time was observed. All changes were perceived more as a cyclical rotation within the familiar frame of things. Niccolò Machiavelli's *The Art of War* (1521) is the last striking example of this view. The otherwise highly perceptive

Florentine failed to recognize the revolutionary effect, already becoming quite apparent during his own time, that firearms were going to have on the conduct of war. On the contrary, he made a point of minimizing their significance, claiming that infantry firearms were no more than a new form of archers and slings, and thus of subsidiary role. Similarly, he regarded artillery as a new form of catapults and ballistae, replacing the latter in siege operations but ineffective on the battlefield.[2] While various explanations have been advanced to explain Machiavelli's glaring failure, it was mainly rooted in his view that no fundamental change in the world and human reality existed—including in war.[3]

However, this classical view of historical reality as basically unchanging was soon to be replaced. A century after Machiavelli, the English philosopher and statesman Francis Bacon argued that the great technologically induced breakthroughs of modernity—firearms, the printing press, and mastery of ocean navigation—had changed human reality in a way never before experienced. By the eighteenth century, the Enlightenment view that humanity was undergoing unprecedented change—known in some of its forms as the idea of Progress—had firmly taken root. This notion deepened further during the nineteenth century, with the Industrial Revolution, the most sweeping transformation of human existence since the transition to agriculture millennia ago. Indeed, from then onward, a succession of technological revolutions has transformed war and its conduct repeatedly and spectacularly. Is there, then, an immutable 'essence' to the phenomenon of war—the supposed foundation of a theory of war and the conduct of military operations—and, if so, what is it?

As mentioned, the military thinkers of the Enlightenment were the first to consider this question. Given the great changes to war and its conduct primarily brought about by the introduction of firearms, they could no longer maintain, as Machiavelli had believed, that the adoption of the battle formations of classical antiquity would be adequate for their own age.[4] At the same time, they were wholly absorbed in the all-encompassing quest of the Enlightenment to form a general theory in each field and discipline—in their case, the military—based on universal rules and principles. But while the patterns of military organization and tactics evidently required adaptation to changing historical conditions, the 'principles' underlying them remained constant. What these underlying principles were was less clear.

Thus, Colonel Jacques Antoine Hippolyte, Comte de Guibert, one of the most prominent military thinkers of the Enlightenment, devised a highly flexible and effective combination of the line and column in the infantry tactical formation. Adopted by the French Royal Army during the last years of the *ancien régime* and inherited by the armies of the Revolution and Napoleon, it would give them a decisive advantage over their rivals.[5] However, rather than regarding tactical formations and doctrines as something inherently dependent on fluctuating historical, mostly technological, developments, Guibert held that they were subject to an underlying, unwavering rationale that needed to be discovered and could be fixed in theory once and for all. Indeed, vague as he remained as to what exactly this rationale was, he implied that his work laid the foundation for it. His view on the matter would sound so strange, if not ridiculous, to us that it is worth quoting at some length precisely because it was deeply representative of his time. As he wrote:

> Almost all sciences have certain or fixed elements, which succeeding ages have only extended and developed, but the tactics, till now wavering and uncertain, confined to time, arms, customs, all the physical and moral qualities of a people, have of course been obliged to vary without end and for a space of a century to leave behind them nothing else but principles disavowed and unpracticed, which have ever been cancelled and destroyed by the following age.[6]

> Let us suppose that the first mathematical truths are taught to people inhabiting the two extremes of the globe… they must evidently in time arrive at the same result of principles. But has there been in the tactics any clear truth demonstrated? Are the fundamental principles of this science established? Has one age ever agreed on this point with its preceding one?[7]

Fortunately, presumably owing to Guibert's book,

> the tactics… would constitute a science at every period of time, in every place, and among every species of arms; that is to say, if ever by some revolution among the nature of our arms which it is not possible to foresee, the order of depth should be again adapted, there would be no necessity in putting the same in practice to change either manoeuvre or constitution.[8]

This was a most typical expression of the Enlightenment worldview applied to the military sphere. A generation later, Antoine-Henri Jomini, the heir of the Enlightenment's military thought, the most successful schematizer of the Napoleonic strategy/art of operations, and the most celebrated and influential military thinker during the first two-thirds of the nineteenth century, shifted the ground only slightly. While accepting that tactics were ever-changing and subject to the conditions of their time, he maintained that at least the principles of strategy were immutable and universal. And yet, the universal validity and applicability of his main strategic precept, the superiority of operating from a central position and on interior lines, was called into question by Napoleon's failed last campaigns, by the latter campaigns of the American Civil War, and by the Prussian campaigns of 1866 and 1870.[9]

The supposedly universal principles of naval warfare advanced by Jomini's disciple Alfred Mahan, highly influential and a huge celebrity in his own right, would be similarly challenged in both theory and practice. His main message, that command of the sea was the key to the world, was derived from the great age of the sail and global ocean travel during the early modern period, covered by his magisterial book *The Influence of Sea Power upon History, 1660–1783* (1890). However, this precept did not remain unaffected by the advent of the railway during the nineteenth century and the resulting shift in balance between sea and land transportation. Mahan overlooked the significance of this sweeping transformation, as it disrupted his belief in a universal theory. The same applied to his advocacy of big battleship supremacy and his downplaying of the revolutionary significance of the newly developed torpedo. Like Machiavelli with respect to firearms, he claimed that the torpedo, an ideal weapon for smaller boats, was the equivalent of, and no more significant than, the fire-ships of old. Mahan equally insisted that commerce raiding as a substitute for the great naval battle was doomed to fail. He believed it contradicted his postulated universal theory as to how naval warfare should be conducted. This had been supposedly demonstrated by France's ultimate defeat in its naval wars with Britain, from the eighteenth century to Nelson. While the universality of Mahan's precepts was challenged in theory by Julian Corbett in *Some Principles of Maritime Strategy* (1911), the German U-boats' commerce raiding campaign, and its torpedo weapon, proved to be the most dangerous threat to the Allied cause in both world wars. As Winston Churchill wrote, this was the only threat that truly worried him during World War II. It might have won the war for Germany had it not been for the enormous industrial capacity of the United States, which dwarfed all others.

As technological change accelerated during the industrial age from the nineteenth century, it became increasingly evident that precepts derived from either Napoleonic warfare on land or Nelson-style warfare at sea were more time- and condition-dependent than both Jomini and Mahan had assumed. All the same, it was deeply felt that there was still some kernel of yet more abstract principles for actions that underlay and ought to guide the conduct of military operations. In the early twentieth century, military theorist J. F. C. Fuller offered such a list of abstract principles that would be adopted in slightly different forms and names by all militaries.[10] These assorted and partly conflicting principles, such as 'the objective', 'concentration of force', 'economy of force', 'initiative', 'surprise', 'cunning', and 'security', have been described by some with slight mockery as 'dazzling flashes of the self-evident'. Still, they have their value as a pedagogic tool and guide for action, for abstraction as well as concreteness are tools that the human mind employs to cope with a complex reality.

INTRODUCTION

The problem of the tension between thin abstractions and thicker, more concrete but historically fluctuating content in creating a substantive theory of war and its conduct was something with which Jomini's contemporary, the Prussian general Carl von Clausewitz, grappled. He was a child of the Romantic Movement or Counter-Enlightenment, the sweeping reaction in Europe, most powerfully raging in Germany, against what people of the time regarded as abstract dogmas of the Enlightenment, insensitive to the specific particularities of different times and places. Clausewitz applied these all-pervasive notions of his cultural milieu to the military field, totally rejecting the Enlightenment's chief concept of universal, abstract principles of war. As he wrote in his twenties and held throughout his life, the theory of strategy 'allows the setting up of few or no abstract propositions'.[11] One cannot escape the multitude of minor circumstances:

> Formula [is] abstraction. When by the abstraction nothing which belongs to the thing gets lost—as is the case in mathematics—the abstraction fully achieves its purpose. But when it must omit the living matter in order to hold to the dead form, which is of course the easiest to abstract, it would be in the end a dry skeleton of dull truths squeezed into a doctrine... precisely that which is the most important in war and strategy, namely the great particularity, peculiarity, and local circumstances, escape these abstractions and scientific systems.[12]

For all that, Clausewitz thought that it might still be possible to formulate a meaningful universal theory of war, sufficiently content-rich to serve as a guide for the actual conduct of military operations. He believed that such a theory could be derived from what he referred to as the unchanging 'nature of war' (he also used the terms 'lasting spirit' and 'concept' of war, interchangeably), validated by experience. He reasonably enough identified the nature of war with the activity of fighting. However, he interpreted this formal definition in very expansive terms, insisting that the nature of war as fighting prescribed total mobilization and the concentration of all forces towards a relentless, all-out effort to crush the enemy in battle. Adhering to this precept, he minimized the significance of major features of war, such as surprise, cunning, and maneuver, which he thought might divert generals and armies away from the imperative of advancing to battle as swiftly as possible.

It must be said that there is nothing in the definition of war as fighting to warrant these radical inferences as to how war ought to be conducted. Clausewitz was so impressed by the scale, energy, and decisiveness of Napoleonic warfare, which dominated his life and times, that he regarded and championed it as the only legitimate form of war. Observing the crushing defeat of all the European great powers before Napoleon and agonizing over the fall of his own Prussia in 1806, he attributed these defeats to the cautious strategy and limited means employed by the powers of the *ancien régime*. He believed these contradicted war's true nature as relentless all-out fighting, which must guide its conduct. Hence, he maintained, their necessary failure in practice.

However, after more than twenty years of forcefully preaching this message, Clausewitz realized that the very core of his ideas was highly questionable. The Spanish and Russian campaigns that paved the way for Napoleon's downfall were characterized by the avoidance of battle, deep withdrawals, scorched earth strategy, and guerrilla warfare on the part of his opponents. All these strategies eschewed direct action to crush the enemy, and yet their outcome was no less momentous than Napoleon's earlier decisive victories. As a result, Clausewitz now felt more deeply than before that a theory of war must encompass all conditions, periods, and forms of war, and not only its crushing Napoleonic form. His interpretation of the nature of war as all-out fighting to energetically destroy the enemy in a decisive battle seemed to fail the 'test of experience', as most of human history evidently did not obey this supposed imperative.

All these thoughts matured to shake Clausewitz to the core in 1827, four years before his death, after he had already finished drafting the first six (out of eight) books of his major work *On War*. With the breakdown of his lifelong view of what the nature of war meant and what it entailed for the conduct of military operations, Clausewitz fell into a deep crisis. He emerged from it by taking a sharp change of course. He now came to the view that limited war was as legitimate as all-out war, and this, he argued, was so primarily because the conduct of war was subject to, dependent on, and shaped by war's political objectives.

Commentators have not recognized that Clausewitz's transformed views about the subordination of the conduct of war to political objectives and his admission of limited war into his theory constituted a U-turn against his own lifelong, most strongly held, and fundamental concept of the nature of war as all-out fighting. It should also be realized that nor was the subordination of the conduct of war to political aims such a novel idea that Clausewitz supposedly pioneered. Understanding the relationship between politics and war had been common in all the great civilizations since ancient times, well-recognized, for example, by Sun Tzu in China, Kautilya in India, and Thucydides in classical Greece. Indeed, it had been the standard in early modern Europe, famously dominated by the principle of *raison d'état* and the practice of limited 'cabinet' wars, which Clausewitz sharply criticized until his latter-day transformation. During the nuclear age, Clausewitz has gained his supposed fatherhood over the subordination of war to politics and the ensuing, revived concept of limited war only because of the century and a half—from Napoleon to World War II—in which all-out, total war and military victory were proclaimed the only legitimate aim in the conduct of war. We will return to this later in the book.

Armed with his new insights, Clausewitz went on to write the last two books of *On War* and planned to revise the first six books of the manuscript that he had written before his intellectual transformation. However, he died after revising the beginning of Book I alone. *On War* as it stood, published posthumously by his widow (1832), thus encompassed both his new ideas in Books I and VIII and his old ones in Books II to VI (except its final chapters). Is it any wonder that readers of the book ever since have found it baffling and been unable to explain to themselves what exactly was going on there? As a result, each period has seen its own strategic outlook in the book: whereas the people of the nineteenth century embraced Clausewitz's imperative of total mobilization and energetic effort to destroy the enemy in battle, in the nuclear age Clausewitz has been hailed for his latter-day insistence on the primacy of the political aim and the idea of limited war. Moreover, reluctant to admit, not least to themselves, that they do not quite understand what exactly is going on in the book, commentators have succumbed to an Emperor's New Clothes syndrome. Faced with the stark contradiction in the unfinished manuscript, whose author changed his mind on the very core of his theory halfway through its writing, they have interpreted Clausewitz's torturous efforts to resolve this contradiction with awe, as an expression of a deep philosophical way of expression.

Another misconception that has taken root among contemporary commentators is that Clausewitz was after a theory of the phenomenon of war, rather than how it ought to be conducted. In truth, as mentioned, he believed that an understanding of the nature of war provided guidance as to how it should be conducted; that this was the main value which made theory worth pursuing. In a note he wrote a few years before his death, he referred to his future book as 'the manuscript on the *conduct* of major operations' [my emphasis]; and his posthumous collected works were also titled *Hinterlassene Werke über Krieg und Kriesgführung* [*On War and the Conduct of War*].[13]

I have written books on all this, to which the interested reader is referred.[14] But rather than explaining Clausewitz or anybody else, our aim in this book is to pick up the threads of the quest that animated both the military thinkers of the Enlightenment and Clausewitz, and has preoccupied many after them—including me, from a very early age, in war-prone Israel. In my work on the history of military thought, my views on the quest to form a universal theory of war have been expressed only obliquely, where at all. It is now time to address the subject head-on. The question to which the book is dedicated is what a theory for the conduct of war is, and, indeed, how general/universal it is, or can be.

INTRODUCTION

In pursuit of its main subject, the book discusses a variety of major themes in the field of strategy, such as the relationship between political aims and military means, what 'victory' is, the relationship between offense and defense, the so-called principles of war, guerrilla warfare, terrorism, the question of whether war is declining, and that of war's relationship to human nature. All of them have been the subject of disagreements and controversy, both in theory and practice. And in all of them, my views are often markedly different from the accepted wisdom. Indeed, much of what appears here relies on, and weaves together in a compact form, my work over the decades on war and military theory.

Thus, the book can act as *both* a 'primer' on strategy for students of war, strategy, and international relations in universities, military colleges, and the public at large *and* engage scholars in these fields. The latter are likely to concern themselves with the book's main argument regarding the nature of military theory, as well as with its associated arguments on the various strategic themes discussed.

Before proceeding, some clarification of our subject is called for. Over time, the meaning of the term 'strategy' has broadened to include not only the actual conduct of war, but also the coordination of all a country's resources—military and non-military—for war, and, further, to the threatening use of power to deter and coerce others without resorting to war. Thomas Schelling's classic books lay the groundwork for this latter investigation.[15] Moreover, the uses of the term 'strategy' have expanded beyond the military field itself, as in political strategy, economic strategy, business strategy, investment strategy, advertising strategy, evolutionary strategy, and even interpersonal or mating strategies. In all these uses, 'strategy' means the optimal application of available means to achieve a desired end. This meaning obviously applies to the military field as well, from which it was originally derived. Indeed, all the broader expansions of the term strategy—military and non-military—aside, this book focuses on the conduct of war itself, on the waging of military operations, on the actual activity of warfare.

1

THE NATURE OF WAR

WHAT CAN BE DERIVED FROM IT FOR THE CONDUCT OF MILITARY OPERATIONS?

Political Objectives and Military Means—
Yet Another Look

By 'war', we mean large-scale, violent, and lethal conflict between human collectives. Since states emerged, gradually spreading across the globe from some 5,000 years ago onward, they have largely monopolized war-making. Thus, Clausewitz famously posited that 'war is nothing but the continuation of policy with other [violent] means'.[1] Some recent critics have suggested that the exclusive identification of war with states does not quite tally with reality, as we increasingly see war waged by non-state actors.[2] The emergence of militant armed organizations such as al-Qaeda and ISIS, Hezbollah and Hamas, and the prospect of unconventional terrorism, have made this observation even more pertinent. Moreover, before the advent of states during historical times, incessant and highly lethal warfare took place between tribes, the highest-level human collectives during the vast extents of prehistory, over tens of thousands and hundreds of thousands of years.[3] In many places, tribes continued to act as agents of war after the emergence of states, and sometimes, where they have survived to the present, they continue to do so. Furthermore, within and around states, other power holders—powerful aristocratic retinues, local militias and their leaders, rogue generals with their armies, freelance mercenary groups, bandits, and pirates—often successfully challenged the state's claim to monopoly over the legitimate use of force. Thus, Clausewitz's identification of war with a unified state policy and subordinate, organized, state armed forces most closely reflected the period in which he lived, when states' hold over the activity of war was at its highest. This period stretched from the eighteenth century onward, under both the absolutist monarchy and modern mass society, soon to become industrial mass society.

While Clausewitz's famous dictum is thus revised and broadened, its basic logic remains clear enough: human collectives may use violence and go to war to attain desired objectives (for simplicity, we shall call them 'political' throughout). Elsewhere, I have extensively addressed the question of what these objectives and the causes of war in general are, a subject poorly covered and often misconceived in the scholarly literature.[4] But this major topic falls outside the scope of the present book, which deals with the conduct of military operations. For this particular interest it is sufficient to revisit Clausewitz's elucidation of the relationship between the military means and the ends they are intended to serve—a relationship that permeates the activity of war.

This fundamental relationship is not institutional but logical. Let me explain: with greater or lesser success, sovereigns always claimed the authority to decide what the desired objectives of the collective should be. Yet Clausewitz, for example—the military man—defied his monarch on some crucial political decisions during Prussia's struggle against Napoleon, and he was not the first or last to have done so. In modern democracies, authority is constitutionally invested in the elected government, which in most cases possesses wide legitimacy and is more or less able to exercise this authority over the objectives and conduct of war. All the same, what concerns us here is not the normative-legal-institutional arrangements of any particular society as to who has the supreme authority, but the implications of the intrinsic relationship between means and ends in the conduct of war. As Clausewitz very well saw, this relationship is a two-way street. As with any means–ends relationship, this logically implies that the ends should guide the use of the military means, but also that the means for the attainment of the desired ends should exist or can be created. The latter aspect of this equation is often less well understood than the former.

Here is a fictitious example. I am an Israeli, so suppose the Israeli cabinet convenes and directs Israel's armed forces to prepare for the conquest of China, to be launched in a year's time. If this objective sounds too ambitious, say the conquest of India. Now, clearly, assuming the Israeli military authorities know their business, they would reply that Israel does not have the means to conquer China, or India, not in a year—or thirty—and that the country and its armed forces are not up to it. The means for such a venture do not exist, nor can they be created. (No country probably has the means to succeed in this particular venture.) It logically follows that if they do not want to fail, Israel's political authorities must revise their policy aims and set other goals. This example is deliberately fanciful for effect, but in a less exaggerated form, these are the kinds of questions and interactions that are central to the setting of policy objectives and shaping of military operations. To succeed, the desired ends and the means to achieve them must be in harmony with each other.

Some cardinal practical questions involved here have created a lot of stir over the past two centuries. Generals, starting most famously with the elder Helmut von Moltke, chief of the Prussian General Staff, have resented the 'meddling' of the political authorities (Bismarck) in the conduct of military operations during the Franco-Prussian

War (1870–1871). To the extent that this means uninformed intervention that is harmful to the cause, their objections are understandable. However, the generals of all the great powers during World War I went as far as barring their respective governments from involvement in, and often knowledge of, their strategic planning, which they claimed belonged to their exclusive professional domain. In Germany, during the latter phase of World War I, generals Hindenburg and Ludendorff practically monopolized the leadership of the war; in Britain, Prime Minister David Lloyd George had a running battle with the generals to reassert his government's authority over the conduct of the war; and in France, Prime Minister Georges Clemenceau, engaging in a similar battle, famously declared that 'war is too important to be left to the generals.' The counter-argument may be that war is too important to be left to the politicians, with their petty interests and uninformed interferences. Inevitably, both politicians and generals have had their fair share of mistakes and biases in the conduct of wars. Again, in the democracies, the supreme authority is clearly invested in the elected government. But rather than on the constitutional-institutional issue—the question of who gets to decide on what—our focus here is on the intrinsic 'logical', two-way-street relationship between means and ends, and its application to the conduct of war. This leads us to the meaning of the major concept of 'victory'.

MILITARY THEORY AND THE CONDUCT OF WAR

What Is Victory in War?

During the last stage of World War II, General Dwight Eisenhower, supreme Allied commander in Europe, rejected all the requests, mostly made by Churchill and the British, that he direct Allied forces in a way that would maximize the Western Allies' territorial advance in Germany and Central Europe, ahead of the Soviets. Eisenhower insisted that his sole mission was to bring about a swift victory over Germany at the smallest cost to his troops, rather than pursue some 'political' objectives belonging to the post-war reality. Although his argument was theoretically flawed, as military operations are supposed to serve a country's political objectives both during and after the war, the reason behind Eisenhower's response was weightier than the question of theoretical clarity. He was following his government's line, which sought good relations with the Soviets in the post-war world, did not accept Britain's balance-of-power politics, and suspected its imperial intentions. To what extent President Roosevelt's view of the post-war world order was misconceived is a different question, which is not our concern here. The more significant theoretical *cum* practical question is revealed in a yet more famous incident: the clash between General Douglas MacArthur and President Truman during the Korean War.

With the United Nations, mostly American, forces pushed back by China's entry into the war, ultimately leading to a stalemate, the frustrated MacArthur demanded that all means, including the employment of nuclear weapons against China, be used to achieve victory. Both the US chiefs of staff and the president, apprehensive of an escalation into a nuclear war with the Soviet Union, rejected his demand. As MacArthur campaigned for his views with the public, in defiance of the president, he was sacked by Truman. This episode, including both its constitutional and strategic elements, has been told repeatedly. And it is MacArthur's statement during the public debate, 'In war there is no substitute for victory', that serves as a starting point for our discussion around what the concept of victory means.

The intuitive meaning of victory that people share is that the enemy's ability to fight is crushed, and as a result he must succumb to the victor's will. Thus, the crushing of the enemy's fighting ability and the attainment of the war's political objectives seem to be intrinsically connected, with the former being a condition for the latter. This was the common perception during the nineteenth and first half of the twentieth century, which MacArthur eloquently expressed. It seemed to follow that the military's task was to complete the job, employing the best means and professional skills at their disposal—at which point the political objectives should take over. Hence the military's demand for autonomy in the planning and execution of military operations to crush the enemy during a war. However, after a century and a half—from 1800 to 1945—during which all-out war dominated in both theory and practice, the intricate, more complex connection between battlefield successes and the attainment of political objectives was to be rediscovered. This intricate connection goes beyond the familiar notion of a 'Pyrrhic victory', a victory which is won at the price of unsustainable losses that weaken the supposed victor.

Note that we have a second intuition regarding what victory in war means, less deeply entrenched than the first, but still clear enough. According to this intuition, victory means the attainment of the desired political objectives. And these two meanings—crushing the enemy's power of resistance and the attainment of the political objectives—have turned out not to be as fully compatible and congruent as previously believed. Clausewitz became more aware of this during the latter phase of his work on *On War*, but the realization was fully developed in theory only a century later by the British military thinker Basil Liddell Hart. As he stressed, a crushing military result may not always serve the political objectives and, indeed, may sometimes be detrimental to them. He called this the 'mirage of victory'.[5]

It took time for this realization to sink in. History is full of examples of such a mismatch, and here is a recent one to illustrate the point. In the first Gulf War (1990–1991), following Iraq's invasion and conquest of Kuwait, the Coalition Forces, with the United States as their mainstay, quickly defeated the Iraqi armed forces and liberated Kuwait. President George H. W. Bush then announced the end of military operations. At the time, some questioned his decision, asking why this spectacular battlefield success was not followed by a drive to Baghdad and the toppling of Saddam Hussein, which could have been easily achieved militarily. Yet the 1991 logic of self-restraint would become apparent during the aftermath of the Second Gulf War. The American invasion of Iraq under President George W. Bush (2003) decisively routed the Iraqi armed forces, Baghdad was taken, and Saddam Hussein's regime was toppled. However, the United States then found itself bogged down in Iraq for years, until the formal end of the occupation (2011), and after. The ethnic cleavages in the country between the Sunni elite, the Shia majority, and the Kurdish provinces, previously kept under the lid by tyrannical regimes, made Iraq barely governable; guerrilla warfare harassed and exacted a bloody toll from the US forces; and the financial costs of occupation mounted. Moreover, by destroying Iraq as a regional power, the American invasion unmade the balance of power in the oil-rich Gulf region. Whereas up until then, Iran and Iraq had balanced each other out, Iran's dominance now remained unchecked and proved to be a much greater potential threat than Iraq.

Not only a less decisive military outcome but also a military draw or even a setback may prove more beneficial in terms of a war's overall results. Again, one example will suffice to illustrate the point. After Israel's spectacular victory in the 1967 Six-Day War, the 1973 Yom Kippur War between Israel and the Arab coalition led by Egypt and Syria ended in a draw of sorts. Following the Arab surprise attack and major successes in the initial stages of the war, Israel repulsed the Syrian invasion and took the war into Syria, but was unable to drive Syria out of the war. On the Egyptian front, the Israeli forces ultimately succeeded in encircling the Egyptian Third Army. But, exhausted and held back by the intervention of the superpowers, skillfully maneuvered by US Secretary of State Henry Kissinger, Israel was not allowed to complete the job. Thus, although Israel succeeded in reversing the course of the war and was spared defeat, the indecisive outcome and heavy human and economic cost of the war were regarded as a major setback and caused deep trauma in the country. In retrospect, however, the more even outcome of the war looks very different. As Kissinger foresaw, it paved the way for the interim agreements between Egypt and Israel, ultimately followed by a peace treaty (1979) that ended three decades of war. Thus, the indecisive end of the war proved politically advantageous for both sides.

A few comments are in order. First, it needs to be clarified that the above examples, like any presented in this book, should be regarded as illustrations only. Realworld situations are complex and complicated, and long-term outcomes are varied, multi-faceted, and often contradictory.

Thus, the intention here is not to issue a definitive verdict on historical cases, which in many ways do not allow for any 'definitive' verdicts. Rather than being committed to any particular interpretation of the above cases, we present them only to illustrate a point. We might as well have used fictitious, imagined examples.

Second and relatedly, it is almost superfluous to say that the objectives in war can and often do change over time, as the sides adjust and change their expectations in view of unfolding situations. Moreover, as we have seen, perspectives on the outcome of wars and on victory may themselves change over time, and change again, as new circumstances emerge. While the military course of a war that ended is ostensibly 'fixed' in the past, assessments of its long-term outcome can be more fluid in many cases. Zhou Enlai, the premier of China under Mao, reportedly replied in 1972 when asked about his opinion on the French Revolution: 'It is too early to say'. Regarded in the West as a partly entertaining, partly sublime example of the long view of ancient Chinese wisdom, it later turned out that Zhou was actually referring to the student demonstrations in Paris 1968 rather than 1789. Still, his saying is too precious to give it up due to historical technicalities. And in our case, it again helps to illustrate the fluidity of the notion of victory over time.

There are other possible standards for 'victory' that people employ interchangeably—for example, measuring the actual political and military outcome of a war against the initial expectations before its outbreak.⁶ Rather than possessing some fixed meaning, concepts—including 'victory'—are adaptable, interpretive, context-dependent cognitive frameworks that help us make sense of and cope with a complex reality. Indeed, our theoretical investigation of both the means–ends relationship and the notion of victory has clear practical implications as leaders and armed forces set out to conceive, plan, and carry out warlike actions. It generates practical insights for the conduct of military operations, emanating, so to speak, from the 'nature of war' and, either positively or negatively, demonstrated in—awakened in our consciousness through—historical experience.

War as Adversarial and Violent— and the Rationale of Military Operations

Additional guiding precepts for the conduct of military operations can be said to flow, more or less, from the nature of war as an adversarial and violent contest between armed collectives over conflicting objectives. Again, Clausewitz elucidated some major such aspects, while misconstruing others. For while some features of the conduct of war are obvious to the point of banality, others are far from being so.

As the activity of fighting is lethal, it is permeated with danger and fear with which those involved in it must cope. Hence the crucial significance of courage, fighting spirit, and morale. Also, to gain the advantage in the violent competition that is war, the sides seek to outsmart one another and thwart their plans. Keeping the other side in the dark or actively deceiving them is a means to this end. Hence the shortage of information and intrinsic uncertainty surrounding war and military operations—the 'twilight' or 'fog of war', and the 'friction' that opens an often wide gulf between military planning and execution. Indeed, given the adversarial nature of military operations, the logic that governs them is non-linear. In the human working of the materials of nature, or in human cooperative ventures—say, in the building of a bridge—it is enough to determine the parameters involved for the project to be realized in a fairly straightforward manner. Even non-violent human competition is normally more subject to regulation of various sorts, which tends to make it more predictable. By contrast, in the violent and largely unregulated activity of fighting, a multiple regression is often involved: you assume I would take line of action A, so I would instead opt for B; but since you think that this is what I might do, I would nevertheless choose A (or C); and so on. Clausewitz saw most of this clearly enough, and Edward Luttwak has further developed the notion of the non-linear logic of military operations.[7]

The guiding rationale of all the above is to maximize the effective force that one brings to bear on the enemy, while minimizing that of the other side. How is this to be achieved? Famous military theorists held contrasting views on this question. As mentioned, Clausewitz, deeply impressed by Napoleon's crushing victories over all the other European great powers, insisted that the nature of war demanded the maximum concentration of force and the most energetic and aggressive conduct, single-mindedly aiming at the destruction of the enemy in a decisive battle. In this light, Clausewitz defined strategy as 'use of the battle/clash of forces [*Gefecht*] for the purpose of the war'.[8] Liddell Hart and others have criticized this definition for positing the battle as the exclusive means of the conduct of war.[9] Moreover, Clausewitz, concerned that wrong ideas and human weakness might distract generals and armed forces from the imperative of advancing as quickly and directly as possible to the battle, consistently belittled the significance of central pillars of warfare such as the maneuver, surprise, and cunning.

Thus, Clausewitz maintains that 'by its very nature [surprise] can rarely be *outstandingly* successful. It would be a mistake, therefore, to regard surprise as a key element of success in war'.[10] As for cunning, consider Clausewitz's quite amazing statement: 'However much one longs to see opposing generals vie with one another in craft, cleverness, and cunning, the fact remains that these qualities do not figure prominently in the history of war… The reason for this is obvious… strategy is exclusively concerned with battles [*Gefechte*]'.[11] The very same view stands behind Clausewitz's suspecting attitude towards the maneuver, both the strategic and tactical.[12] All these notions lead to Clausewitz's surprisingly dull description of battle. No maneuvers or stratagems are portrayed. The only image conveyed is of a direct, gray clash of physical and moral masses.[13]

Clausewitz's views went against the central precept, practiced throughout history (including, of course, by Napoleon himself) and most notably developed in the field of theory by Sun Tzu and Liddell Hart: that success in the conduct of military operations depended on a prior psychological and physical dislocation and undermining of the enemy—throwing him off balance—by the crafty use of maneuver, surprise, and cunning. This, according to Liddell Hart in his *Strategy: The Indirect Approach*, meant choosing the lines of least expectation and least resistance.[14] Head-on clashes all too often result in mutual massacres and few substantive results.

As Clausewitz overemphasized direct force, while Liddell Hart's important correction may have been somewhat overdrawn, their precepts are best viewed in tandem. What Machiavelli argued with respect to politics applies even more to the conduct of military operations: to be most effective, the belligerents must combine the qualities of the lion and the fox—be both strong and crafty.[15] These qualities complement each other, and both are very real factors necessary for success in war. Yet there is also tension between them: under what circumstances to tilt more towards either resolute force or cunning evasion.

Much the same applies to the lists of the so-called principles of war adopted during the twentieth century by most militaries. As mentioned earlier, the notion of universal principles of war that would transcend the diversity and transformation of war and its conduct was pioneered by the military thinkers of the eighteenth-century Enlightenment. Yet, contrary to their pretense, their efforts in this regard turned out to be mostly time-bound, actually reflecting the particular forms of war prevalent in their times, as well as being of partial validity. In the wake of the sweeping, predominantly technology-induced transformations of the industrial age, from the nineteenth century onward, the phrase and concept of 'principles of war', stemming from the Enlightenment, have been retained. But it has taken the very abstract formulation familiar today. However, it is precisely the very abstract form of these 'principles' that raises the problem over which Clausewitz agonized, as we have seen.[16] So-called universal principles, he wrote, might either be full of concrete content relevant to particular forms of war, but at the price of being historically transitory and one-sided; or they can be so abstracted from specific content reflecting thick concrete conditions that they become almost empty and lose their value as guidance for action. The current lists of abstract principles do not escape this problem. Still, while they have been criticized as banal by many, it is widely felt by others that they possess real educational value, distilling and focusing the mind on genuine elements that should guide the conduct of military operations. Both views are not without merit.

The US list of 'principles of war' includes the following: Objective; Offensive; Mass; Economy of Force; Maneuver; Unity of Command; Security; Surprise; Simplicity. The lists of other militaries differ slightly in both names (semantics) and by the inclusion or exclusion of some of the principles. We need not bother too much about these differences or about any exact formulation of the principles. These are not the Ten Commandments, and even in them God could have benefited from a good editor. Like the Ten Commandments, they are practical precepts, and the marked convergence between the various lists suggests that they capture something sufficiently meaningful to be of value. Nor shall we dwell here on the well-known tensions that exist between the various 'principles of war'. For example, take the central principle of the 'concentration of force', which the US Army calls 'mass'. Liddell Hart, for one, borrowing from the naval theorist Julian Corbett, argued that in order to leave the enemy in the dark and force him to disperse his forces and span of attention, the attacker himself should adopt calculated dispersion, prior to a rapid concentration of forces at the moment and point of his attack.[17]

We shall similarly limit our bickering on the titles of the principles to one example. The US principle of 'offensive' actually means, or should mean, initiative and aggressive-vigorous conduct, as the first sentence elaborating this principle indeed has it: 'Seize, retain, and exploit the initiative'. As Machiavelli suggests in *The Prince* (chapter 25), by seizing the initiative, one is able to steer and dictate the course of events, be a step ahead of the other side, keep them guessing, and force them to dance to one's tune. Machiavelli argues that seizing the initiative and acting vigorously also helps one cope more effectively with chance (fortune). Those who formulated the principle of Offensive in the US military could not have meant that US forces should never take a defensive stance—implemented dynamically and vigorously. Even for a superpower this would be very unwise. It is not necessary here to dwell on the many historical examples in which masterful defense has been both opportune and highly advantageous. The Duke of Wellington was one famous exponent of the defensive battle, in both the Iberian Peninsula, against Napoleon's marshals, and at Waterloo, against the emperor himself.

This takes us to a major fundamental distinction in the theory and practice of war: that between defense and attack.

Defense and Attack: Is the Defense the Stronger Form; or Is Offense the Best Defense?

While there are many ways to characterize defense and attack, the one that seems to best reflect the root of these concepts analytically is their relation to the status quo. The defense aims to preserve the status quo, whereas the offense aims to change it. Clausewitz made this point clearly enough. As he wrote, 'Defence has a negative [*negativ*] purpose: *preservation*; and attack a positive one: *conquest*'.[18] He specifically referred to their opposite orientation vis-a-vis the 'status quo'.[19] At the same time, Clausewitz was in the wrong about most of the rest he attributed to defense and attack in his extensive treatment of them.

We are already familiar with the source of his mistake. He posited aggressive conduct, relentlessly leading to the decisive battle, as the only legitimate form of war, flowing from its very nature as fighting. He thus 'needed' an intellectual counterbalance if defense—characterized by the opposite traits of waiting and parrying—was to make any sense at all. The counterbalance he came up with was the idea that 'the defensive form of warfare is intrinsically stronger than the offensive'.[20] According to his logic: 'If attack were the stronger form, there would be no case for using the defensive, since its purpose is only negative [*negativ*]. No one would want to do anything but attack; defence would be pointless'.[21] All the rest of Clausewitz's arguments on the subject are intended to support and are subordinate to his logical premise. But this logic is invalid. For example, Clausewitz writes:

> If defence… has a negative object, it follows that it should be used only so long as weakness compels and be

abandoned as soon as we are strong enough to pursue a positive object… It would therefore contradict the very concept [*Begriff*] of war to regard defence as its final purpose. [22]

Exceptional among the chorus of recent commentators for whom Clausewitz could simply not be wrong, Raymond Aron, sharing the West's defensive, status quo-oriented, and political posture of Containment during the Cold War, writes: 'Whoever repulses the enemy and keeps what the enemy wanted to take, imposes his will on him.' Why then should he 'give himself another goal?' Why must the defender go over to the attack? Why cannot the defense be the final aim in war?[23]

In the end, Clausewitz himself came to recognize this point, which, four years before his death, generated a revolution in his entire work. He found it necessary to allow the concept of a 'defence which does not seek a decision' into his theory of war.[24] As he realized, 'The negative aim, which lies at the heart of pure resistance, is also the natural formula for outlasting the enemy, for wearing him down.'[25] This, indeed, is also the formula behind guerrilla warfare that drew Clausewitz's attention following its major successes against Napoleon in both Spain and Russia.[26] By merely enduring, the defender may frustrate the attacker's efforts, compel him to withdraw from the war, and thus maintain the status quo.[27] The defender 'reaps where he did not sow.'[28] Here, the advantage of defense derives, so to speak, from the concept of defense itself, aiming at preserving, and being satisfied with, the status quo.

Still, other major missteps that Clausewitz took in his treatment of defense and attack remained. I have analyzed elsewhere his rather convoluted efforts to prove that defense is *intrinsically* and *universally* stronger than the attack.[29] Here we shall only cite some of the arguments he made to the extent that they may reflect notions more broadly shared by others who ponder the question of what the 'nature' of defense and attack is. Our investigation involves some abstract reasoning which is necessary to clarify the issue.

Strong intuitions tend to support the view that defense is the stronger form of war. As Clausewitz wrote, one of its chief advantages, which 'arises solely from the nature of war, derives from the advantage of position, which tends to favour the defence.'[30] Now, historically it is true that, chiefly by hindering movement and providing cover from detection, carefully chosen ground features have indeed tended to benefit the defense on land, both at the operational and tactical levels. Moreover, with the introduction of firearms, the importance of ground features and prepared positions in providing shelter has increased far more than before. However, surprising as this may appear, all these features and historical developments are, so to speak, contingent rather than imminent in war. This can be demonstrated, for example, by sea warfare, about which Clausewitz should have known, not to mention air or space warfare which he could not have foreseen—all of which are much less affected by terrain and by the shelter offered by position. Moreover, with nuclear weapons, for example, defense is almost impossible, while an easily carried out and devastating nuclear attack can be effectively prevented only by deterrence, or by the threat of a similar, practically unstoppable, attack. Let the argument be clear: the point is not that Clausewitz failed to anticipate nuclear weapons, but that he confused some historically prominent, yet contingent factors of land warfare with what flows—or can be deduced—from the 'nature of war' itself.

Another reason why people tend to regard the offensive as being at a disadvantage is that it is often associated—including, for example, in naval and air warfare—with the challenge of, and logistical problems involved in, crossing distances, sometimes of great length. For all these reasons, people sometimes still repeat the World War I trench warfare formula that, other things being equal, the attacker needs to have a three to one numerical advantage over the defender in order to succeed. Yet this is just a shibboleth, contradicted whenever initiative, mobility, and surprise give the offense the upper hand. Indeed, should not initiative and surprise, which also promise superior concentration of force, be regarded as being more closely associated with the attack, possibly counterbalancing the advantage accorded to the defense by factors that might be more closely associated with it?

The one-sidedness of Clausewitz's treatment of the subject is demonstrated by some often cited concepts he coined, such as 'the diminishing force of the attack' and 'the culminating point of attack.' They both seem to strike a chord in people's minds as genuine features of reality. However, for a more balanced picture, could one not offer, for example, a concept such as 'the breaking point of defense', after which we know empirically that the defeated suffers most of its losses? As for 'the diminishing force of the attack', it undoubtedly occurs in many cases—Clausewitz was deeply impressed by the fact that in Napoleon's 1812 Russian campaign: 'Half a million men crossed the Nieman; only 120,000 fought at Borodino, and still fewer reached Moscow.'[31] All the rest of the French troops were stretched across and defending Napoleon's long lines of communication. That said, Clausewitz himself argued that the attack 'increases one's own capacity to wage war' by *expanding* one's resources, whereas the defense 'does not'.[32]

So which is it? Does the strength of the attack diminish over time, or does it increase with the expansion of the resources at its disposal, which at the same time might be lost to the defender? This is where we reach the crux of the matter and Clausewitz's fundamental mistake. The power relationship between offense and defense is not *intrinsic* and *universal*. In some cases, under specific circumstances, the defense may possess greater advantages, while in other cases and under other circumstances, offensive action might offer greater advantages—even for the weaker side. For example, the advantages derived from the use of initiative, mobility, and surprise might serve as a force multiplier for the attacker. After all, there is a reason why a well-known maxim proclaims that 'offense is the best defense'. Do not misunderstand: I do not think this maxim is necessarily or universally true either, but only that differing circumstances alter the power balance between defense and attack.

I suspect that many readers might be wary of so much abstract reasoning, so here are a few concrete historical examples. For other works of mine, I have done extensive research on pre-state warfare during our prehistoric past. It turns out that the most common and most effective method of fighting then was the night raid on a sleeping camp or dwellings of another tribe, which often resulted in wholesale massacre. Thus, initiative and surprise were the key to success in pre-state warfare, which made the offensive that much more effective and the defense so helpless and disadvantageous. Lest it be thought that for whatever reason prehistory is irrelevant, note that the same applies to any case where conditions favor pre-emptive or first-strike action.

The following is another example, regarding grand strategy. During the Second Punic War (218–202 BCE), both sides, Rome and Carthage, were most vulnerable at home and on the defense. The reason for this was that the power of both derived from their imperial domains of subject satellite peoples that provided both troops and resources. In both the Roman imperial domain in Italy and that of Carthage in North Africa and Spain, many of these satellite peoples were eager to break free. A successful invader thus threatened the very foundations of the other side's power. For this reason, both Rome and Carthage sought to conduct the war in the other's territory. Hannibal succeeded in being the first to invade, and his crushing battlefield victories in Italy, again holding the initiative and using cunning and surprise, indeed led to a defection of many of Rome's subject 'allies' and put Rome in its greatest danger ever. His final defeat only came when Rome was eventually able to turn the tables and invade, first Spain and later North Africa, triggering a massive defection of Carthage's subject peoples.

There is no need to go on with this and cite the numerous historical examples in which taking the initiative and the employment of mobility and surprise gave the advantage to the attacker at either the tactical or strategic levels, or both, and sometimes even when the attacker was the weaker side. In such cases the offense indeed proved to be the best defense. We shall not belabor the point any further.

In each period or set of circumstances, many changing factors—some more enduring than others—shape the face of war and determine the relationship between defense and attack. This relationship has gone through several alternations during the last two centuries—mostly technologically induced. Thus scholars in the fields of international relations and security, having become more relativist in their approach, have come to view the balance between defense and attack in more circumstantial historical terms.[33] They tend to see it more as subject to the development of weapons systems and counter-systems than to intrinsic and universal traits arising from the very nature of the two modes of warfare.

Having said all this, maybe the point is not that the defense is intrinsically and universally stronger than the attack, but that it is easier to carry out because it can succeed, for example, with fewer trained troops and may require less sophisticated tactics and less proficiency in implementing them. This clearly applies to a vast span of historical experience, though, as we have seen, the opposite is the case, for example, with nuclear weapons. Indeed, it is time to pause for a moment and try to establish more clearly what it means for various traits—those we have considered and will consider—to belong to the 'nature of war' and what this implies for our understanding of what constitutes a theory for the conduct of military operations.

How to Determine What Is in the 'Nature of War'— and What Is Historically Shaped and Transitory?

Up until now we have discussed the 'nature of war' without explaining what this concept could mean. It seemed better to begin this book with some major substantive questions regarding the theory of war and its conduct, rather than by probing deep into very abstract questions that many readers might find inaccessible or of lesser immediate interest. Now, however, having accumulated some mileage in our discussion of what could be deduced from the 'nature of war', it is time to devote a few pages to elucidating our usage of this concept.

The first thing to clarify is that all concepts—including 'war'—are cognitive frameworks coined by the human mind to make sense of an infinitely complex and ever fluctuating reality. Our minds group together and tag phenomena that are similar enough but never identical—no war (or house, or tree) is identical with any other. We alter these framings, adjust their conceptual boundaries, and split them into sub-framings whenever we find it helpful and effective for coping with an infinite and changing reality. As the cognitive device of conceptualization is built into us, people tend to confuse the concepts with the things they represent. This gives rise to endless semantic arguments over, for example, what Islam 'truly' is, or whether movies are an art form or a business, or whether something (say, a major cyber attack) should 'really' count as war.[34] All these questions can have various diverging and/or complementary answers, depending on the circumstances and our perspectives and interests. Thus, war itself is a concept whose boundaries and what they reflect depend on some rough semantic agreement. For example, does war encompass tribal or other non-state fighting, intense and extremely lethal as it often is, or should the concept be limited to where large and organized armies at the service of centralized states are involved? While such distinctions are obviously very significant and sometimes deserve careful elaboration, there is no 'correct' delineation of the conceptual boundaries of definitions per se; there is no 'essence' to things except as a useful human construct—which does not stop people from very seriously and pedantically arguing about them. The definitions themselves are in flux, chasing after a fluctuating and complex reality. Consider, for example, that the root of the English word war is Old Frankish-German *werra*, going back to a tribal, pre-state past and meaning confusion, discord, or strife—not very far from what Thomas Hobbes meant by his primordial 'warre'.

That said, once a rough semantic agreement on the use of a particular definition is accepted by those participating in the discourse, various analytical distinctions and features within the concepts can be elucidated. This includes what people refer to, as I do—always within quotation marks—as the 'nature of war'. Such analytical distinctions, 'by definition', are traditionally regarded by philosophers as formal and empty in the sense that they add no new content or information to what is already implicit in the original concept. Still, as we have seen, they may be of great value, illuminating significant features of the phenomenon in question that are not always clear or self-evident and may sometimes have very practical implications for the real world.

We have discussed some major such features and their practical implications. The relationship between 'political' ends and 'military' means in war is logically derived from what the concepts of ends and means signify in general. Understood by Clausewitz but often missed in references to this relationship, including by those who cite Clausewitz in this regard, is the fact that the means–ends relationship is a two-way street. This means that for the 'political' ends to be realized, they should shape the scope and direction of the 'military' means employed; but, by the same token, it also means that the properties and availability of the means at hand must necessarily affect the process of determining and framing the ends themselves—again, if the ends are to be within the realm of the achievable.

A cardinal aspect of the ends-means relationship concerns the notion of victory and what it signifies. Once more, this can be analytically derived from the 'nature of war', while nonetheless being far from self-evident or well-recognized. On the contrary, what victory means has been the source of major practical differences of salient historical significance during recent centuries. The deep-seated notion that victory meant crushing the enemy's ability to resist has often led to active resistance by the military to political 'interference' in the conduct of war. Moreover, 'in war there is no substitute for victory' is a slogan that has also resonated with the public at large. It took some bitter experiences to bring out what is analytically implicit in the 'nature of war' itself: that the crushing of the enemy is not necessarily the best military means for achieving the desirable political end and shaping the *aftermath* of a war—that it could often be counter-productive; that rather than viewed as a self-contained phenomenon, war is, and should be treated as, part of a broader and longer continuum in the overall frame of military means and political ends espoused by those waging it.

The distinction and relationship between defense and attack is another major example of what can and cannot be analytically inferred from the 'nature of war' and of the potentially non-trivial practical implications of such inferences. As we have seen, the distinction between these two forms of war is best characterized by their respective relation to the status quo: one aims to preserve it, while the other aims to change it. Clausewitz got this right, while getting everything else wrong about the subject, which only demonstrates how slippery and error-prone analytical distinctions and their practical implications can be. The defense should not necessarily be adopted only by the weaker side, who, moreover, must switch to the attack once they become stronger. Choices in this regard are decided by one's overall aims and cost-benefit calculations. Nor is defense intrinsically and universally stronger than the attack. True, a draw, which preserves the status quo, ipso facto favors the defense. Otherwise, the power relations between defense and attack, rather than being anchored in the 'nature of war', depend on a variety of circumstances and factors—some of which, under certain conditions, can work in favor of the defense and some in favor of the attack.

Other central features of war that we have seen, while not *analytically* deduced from the 'nature of war', are still very closely associated with it. They consist of very strong propensities linked to the activity of fighting as an adversarial and deadly contest. We mentioned features such as the element of fear in the face of the danger of death, which calls for the qualities of courage, fighting spirit, or morale; the 'fog of war'; the non-linear logic of the conduct of military operations; the combined significance of brute force, cunning, deception-surprise, and similar means to throw the other side off balance; initiative, and a resolute and vigorous/bold action, which should not become recklessness; and a similarly applied balancing act between sticking to the objective and flexibility, and between concentration of force, economy of force, and security. Other features may be added to the list.

All of the above are elementary in both senses of the word: all of the features described are either analytically derived from the 'nature of war' or very closely associated with it. Some of them are obvious to the point of banality, while others turn out to be far less so.

Is there more to the theory of the conduct of war beyond this? Yes, there is—a great deal—but rather than being universal, the bulk of this theory consists of historically-bound practices and doctrines: of long, medium, or short-range validity.

2

HISTORY AND MILITARY DOCTRINE

The quest for and fascination with the universal has held a special place in the human psyche, at the very least since the beginning of Greek philosophy. The military thinkers of the eighteenth-century Enlightenment, having become conscious of the historical transformation of human reality, nonetheless sought to discover universal rules and principles that transcended all change. Clausewitz, living through and expressing the rise of the current of thought known as 'historicism', was even more aware of diversity and change while agonizing over what this meant for the feasibility and scope of a universal theory of war and its conduct. We shall not go again into his answer to this question and the deep problems in which he found himself because of it. We shall only point out, as commentators have occasionally and forgivingly remarked, that much (indeed, the bulk) of *On War* actually deals with the details and features of armies and war during the eighteenth and early nineteenth centuries. In other words, much of this thick volume is time-bound and now wholly outdated. Clausewitz simply did not realize the huge potential for the transformation of armed forces and war as was very soon to kick in with the Industrial Revolution and the consecutive and rapid technologically-induced military revolutions it brought in its wake. His failure here was not primarily one of imagination—the historically unprecedented scale of the changes was practically impossible to predict. Again, his was more a failure in the rigorous application of logic as to what was truly 'intrinsic' and 'unchanging' in the 'nature of war'.

Indeed, most of the practical know-how concerning the conduct of war, codified into theory, is time-bound and intimately associated with the particular broad conditions of the era concerned. From the twentieth century onward, such theorizing has increasingly been referred to as 'doctrine'. This term was adapted from older, mostly religious uses in Christianity, in which it signified the Church's official guidelines to the believers (*docere* in Latin = to teach). Contrary to notions that may prevail among the theoretically inclined, there is nothing inferior or second-rate in these parts of theory because of their transitory character. Rather, they are by far the real stuff from which professional expertise in military affairs is made. Doctrines abstract and generalize the most salient features of a particular form of fighting, in a particular technological, social, and political epoch—long, medium, or short—which then inform and guide the conduct of war.

The 'Levels' of the Conduct of War

All this also applies to much that is perceived as fundamental concepts in the theory of war. The terms strategy and tactics, constructed from ancient Greek, were only sporadically used in various contexts in European military literature before the second half of the eighteenth century. They then became standard, distinguishing between two so-called 'levels' of the conduct of war.[1] While strategy referred to the overall shaping of a war and of campaigns, tactics dealt with the actual clash of forces, mostly, though not exclusively, on the battlefield, where armies met on a relatively small area of a few square miles for a fight lasting a day or so, which often decided the fate of the war.

These features of fighting reflected millennia of state warfare, characterized by large, organized armies, long-distance campaigning, complex logistics, and much else. They applied less to the vast time span of prehistoric, pre-state, tribal warfare, for example. Still, it is characteristic of the 'essentialist'-'metaphysical' frame of mind to think of terms such as strategy and tactics as fundamental, fixed, and everlasting, rather than evolving, conceptual frames that are useful for their time.

Consider the additional 'levels' in the conduct of war, the formulation of which has been found necessary and useful as war and its conduct have undergone massive transformations since the beginning of industrial modernization after 1815. As armies expanded greatly in size and, moreover, spaced out to counter the effect of steeply growing firepower, they spread and fought across vast theaters of war, rather than marching and fighting in a close formation as before. It was to reflect this new reality that a new 'level' and term were coined and have gradually become accepted from the late nineteenth century onward: that of 'operations'.

Military theorist Georgi Isserson, one of the leading pioneers of the Soviet doctrine of 'operational art' and 'deep battle', very clearly understood the historical context in which this new 'level' in the conduct of war had come into being. His Marxist-historicist approach helped him in this regard, if less so in others. As he wrote: 'The conduct of war in the Napoleonic era consisted schematically of two main stages…: a large, long march, which gave rise to a long operational line, and a short battle concluding it in a single place'. Thus, 'Before the [First] World War military art included two basic parts: strategy, as the study of war, and tactics as the study of the engagement.' However, 'different socio-political conditions, a different arsenal of the technical means of struggle' were among the factors that changed things.

> As early as the second half of the 19th century, the evolution of the forms of armed struggle did not fit into the concepts of strategy and tactics alone; it went beyond their boundaries. Armed struggle gave rise to an entire chain of combat events, spread out along the front and broken up in depth…. These phenomena required a new concept, which

under the name of operational art as the study of the operation, which only following the [First] World War occupied its independent position in a new three-tiered system of dividing military art.²

The fluctuation, adaptation, and expansion of the conceptual schema to keep pace with a transforming reality did not end there. With the advent of 'total war', the term and concept of 'grand strategy' also came into usage after World War I. It was found necessary so as to reflect the new reality in which massive industrial mobilization, mass communications, global conflicts, and other salient features of modern warfare had to be integrated and coordinated. 'Defense policy' is an equivalent term that has become more prevalent after World War II, though the term 'grand strategy' has also survived.

To be sure, these new terms can sometimes be applied to earlier warfare in the same way that, say, 'tactics' (much less so 'strategy')—centering on the night raid and ambush, rather than on battle—is meaningfully applied to prehistoric tribal warfare. Similarly, Edward Luttwak's *The Grand Strategy of the Roman Empire* (1976) uses a concept that is meaningful and valuable enough in the context employed (even if the true nature of Roman grand strategy may be disputed).³ All the same, viewing the various 'levels' in the conduct of war—from minor tactics to grand strategy—as fundamental or fixed brings to mind the fixed seven heavens of ancient cosmology.

Enter the Concept of Doctrine:
Military Revolutions—Past and Present

As noted, the concept of doctrine has entered into wider currency in military affairs in the wake of the Industrial Revolution, as the pace of innovation in military technology has accelerated dramatically in comparison to pre-industrial times. The most significant pre-industrial technological innovations that had affected warfare over the millennia included bronze followed by iron weapons, the warhorse, and some more limited innovations, such as the longbow. But these changes were too slow, far between, and obscured by the mists of pre- and proto-history to be noticeable. To be sure, ancient civilizations had a variety of military practices, regulated orders of battle, drills, and even some literary tracts, to which military manuals of all sorts were added during the early modern period, after the invention of print. However, as we saw with Machiavelli, the last major representative of the classical view of history as basically immutable, the slow pace of change during premodern times made the military institutions and practices of ancient civilizations effectively indistinguishable from their notion of military theory.

Thus, by and large, the phalanx and the way it was employed *was* the Greek theory of war; the practices surrounding legionary warfare *were* basically the Roman theory of war; mobile horseback archery *was* the essence of nomad steppe warfare; much the same applied to knightly warfare during the High Middle Ages; and the maneuver of oared ships *was* what naval warfare meant, replaced by the sailing ship during the early modern period. While practitioners and authors were not unfamiliar with the military institutions and practices of other civilizations they met in war, these normally remained peripheral to their own practice of war and perception of military theory.

Awareness of and sensitivity to change grew during the early modern period, including in military affairs, following the introduction of firearms. And yet what military theory per se meant for both the military thinkers of the Enlightenment and Clausewitz was basically the ideal of the immutable and eternal. Even when engaged in devising the best tactics for musket infantry, the military thinkers of the Enlightenment believed that there were underlying principles to be discovered governing the width and depth of any infantry array or formation—past, present, and future. Indeed, they could not imagine that foot infantry itself was not a fundamental feature of war. There was nothing in known experience that could suggest this, not even to Clausewitz with his greater sensitivity to historical change. Recall that the main infantry weapon, the musket, changed little from 1690 to 1820.

By contrast, during the nineteenth century, the steam engine, rifled and breech-loading guns, and the telegraph revolutionized war to a degree that most observers could not ignore. Even if sometimes belatedly or imperfectly, militaries adapted their field manuals and other regulations to the changes. Still, it was only with the Second Industrial Revolution around 1900—above all the introduction of the internal combustion engine, with the ensuing mechanization of land warfare and the advent of air warfare—that the notion of 'doctrine' for the conduct of these new forms of war became standard in military theory. These technologically-induced revolutions have been widely recognized as epoch-making in the two senses of the phrase: while they revolutionized the conduct of war and attracted universal and intense attention during the first half of the twentieth century, their historically specific nature as a complete novelty was never in question, even if some analogies to cavalry and naval warfare were considered useful for projections of future mechanized forces. 'Doctrine' took its place as something distinct from theory's elevated part codified in the 'principles of war', while supposedly 'implementing' them in each doctrine's particular sphere.

As military theorist J. F. C. Fuller pointed out, sweeping revolutions in warfare followed each other in quick succession from the beginning of the industrial-technological era, closely bound up with the broader revolutions in civilian technology.[4] Although some simplification is necessarily involved, Fuller rightly identified three such major revolutionary waves of civil and military technological change during the nineteenth and twentieth centuries.

The First Industrial Revolution was spearheaded by the steam engine and major advances in metallurgy and machine tools. Applied to the military field, the railway increased armies' strategic mobility and logistical capability by a factor of hundreds. While naval mobility only doubled or tripled as steam replaced sail, iron, and steel battleships' size increased tenfold and more, with their might spiraling yet higher. To these was added the revolution in information communications. Electric telegraph lines connected not only armies across countries but also naval bases across oceans and continents in real time, where weeks, months, and years had once been necessary to convey a message. Simultaneously during the nineteenth century, the revolution in metallurgy and machine tools generated a revolution in firearms and tactics. Rifling and breech loading were pioneered in infantry firearms during the 1840s, and in artillery during the 1850s and 1860s. Magazine-fed rifles, 'repeaters', were developed in the 1860s and 1870s, and quick-firing artillery, using a hydraulic mechanism to absorb the gun's recoil, in the 1880s and 1890s. As a result, range, accuracy, and rapidity of fire increased some tenfold each within sixty years, not counting the development of the automatic machine gun from the 1880s, which multiplied firepower even more.[5] Naval gunnery underwent similar developments, to which the torpedo was added from the 1870s.

As we have seen, in land warfare these developments spread armies over vast theaters of war and prompted decentralized doctrines such as *Auftragstaktik* or mission-oriented tactics, as armies could no longer be kept closely together and directly controlled by the commanding general. Similarly, the conceptualization of the 'operational level' in the conduct of war was devised, respectively, in German and Soviet military theory to adjust to the new realities. Furthermore, Jan Bloch accurately foresaw in his *Future War* (1898; English trans. *Is War Now Impossible?*) that the exponential increase in firepower was going to freeze warfare along continuous lines of trenches. This, he argued, would lead to protracted wars of attrition, with disastrous results for all the powers involved. In naval warfare, the advent of the railway and the torpedo were undermining some of Mahan's most fundamental precepts regarding both the paramountcy of sea power and the supremacy of the capital ship. As we shall see, his theories would soon crack further under yet more pressure from subsequent revolutionary changes. Historical-technological developments proved much more pertinent to the conduct of war than the universalist claims of classical texts.

In the wake of the First Industrial Revolution, while armies rode trains on their way to the battlefield and were easily controlled by telegraph, they still fell from the pinnacle of high-tech communications back to Napoleonic if not Alexandrian times once in the theater of operations and on the battlefield. Their mobility there remained confined to human muscles, with their artillery and supply drawn by horses, of which hundreds of thousands remained in each of the great powers' armies during World War I. Field command and control, if telegraph lines could not be laid in advance, was similarly downgraded to messengers on foot or horseback. Furthermore, whereas firepower increased tenfold and more, troops, while dispersing and taking cover, still had nothing better than their skin to protect them from the storm of steel on the open field. Hence the murderous stalemate on the Western Front during World War I, both tactical and operational, which Bloch had foreseen. Even those puny gains made by attacking infantry at a terrific cost were reversed as decimated foot walking troops, struggling to extend their tactical gains, were pushed back by enemy reinforcements rushed up by rail.

However, from the 1880s, the Second Industrial Revolution was beginning to unfold in civilian life, affecting the military field as profoundly as the First Industrial Revolution had. Chemicals, electric power, and the internal combustion engine dominated that second revolutionary wave. The chemical industry contributed new explosives and was soon to produce chemical warfare. Developments in electricity also had various military applications, including radio communication. But it was the internal combustion engine that affected war the most decisively. It made mobility possible in the open country, away from railways. Automobiles (as well as the tractor) evolved between 1895 and 1905, increasing cross-country mobility by a factor of tens. World War I inaugurated the tank—an armored and armed tractor—which introduced mechanized mobility and mechanized armored protection into the battlefield, thereby redressing the huge imbalance created by steam. Controlled by radio, which similarly extended real-time information communication into the field, away from stationary telegraph lines, mechanized armies on tracks and wheels came into being during the period of the world wars.

The influential, prophetic theorist of the new age of mechanized land warfare, despite some inevitable lapses in his vision, was the British General Fuller. During the interwar period, he was joined by Liddell Hart in Britain and was admired and adopted by Heinz Guderian and the founders of the Panzer arm in Germany, as well as by Charles de Gaulle in France, albeit less successfully. With some significant modifications, pioneering British armored theory and practice also prompted the originators of Deep Battle in the Soviet Union.[6] It was these historically specific doctrines, and their practical implementation, that mattered most in shaping the conduct and outcome of military operations during the period concerned.

Simultaneously, the internal combustion engine also made possible mechanized air flight. A remarkably similar trajectory to land warfare followed, with the first mechanized flight taking place in 1903, and massive air forces quickly coming into being during World War I and further developing by World War II. Giulio Douhet was the most recognized theorist of air power throughout continental Europe and in the United States.[7] But his vision that strategic airpower would supplant all the other services and decide wars within hours or days was to prove much less prescient than Fuller's in land warfare. Ships, already steam-powered and armored, were less dramatically affected by the internal combustion engine. Nonetheless, naval warfare in general was revolutionized. Dual propulsion by the internal combustion and electric engines made possible the first workable submarine, again in 1900. During the two world wars, the submarine belied Mahan's out-and-out rejection of commerce raiding as a viable form of war at sea. In addition, the aircraft was to bring about the demise of the gunned battleship. Together, the submarine and the aircraft completely dominated naval warfare by World War II.

The Third Industrial-Technological or Information Revolution was driven by new technological breakthroughs, primarily in electronics and computers, which again transformed both civilian life and war. Radar, followed by electro-optic, television, lasers, and satellite guidance for missile weapon systems have progressively revolutionized air, sea, air-land, and land battle. Fast-improving sensors of all sorts, in combination with electronic computation capacity that more or less doubled every eighteen months, made the identification, acquisition, and destruction of most hardware targets almost a foregone conclusion, virtually irrespective of range. Showing few signs of leveling off, the electronic revolution is bringing about increasing automation—the electric-robotic warfare that the pioneering Fuller predicted as early as 1928 as the third great wave after mechanization.[8] Moreover, fighting systems are now being increasingly integrated into networks of computation, big data, web communication, and automation. As a result, a Fourth Wave of technological revolution, extending from the Third Wave and centering on cyber networks, now leads military innovation in the conduct of war, both offensively and defensively.

Here are some speculations regarding the face of things to come. These lines are being written as Russia's war with Ukraine is raging. Since the full-scale invasion in 2022, attention has been drawn to the new technologies that have been revolutionizing warfare, such as drones, AI and big data, cyber, automation, and robotics. And yet, a major aspect of the application of the Third-Fourth revolution may have been overlooked.

Note how the electronic revolution has transformed naval and air warfare. At sea, the heavily armored, big-gun capital ships vacated the scene. Naval warfare, whether air, sea, or land borne, is waged offensively by electronic guided missiles and defensively by electronic disruption and interception systems. Similarly, air warfare, once based on the kinetic capabilities of planes and their armament, now relies primarily on electronically guided weapons and electronic defensive systems. The medium in which land warfare takes place is immeasurably more complex than those of sea and air warfare, because of both the numbers of combatants and fighting systems involved and land's topographical features. But at least since the early 1980s, the direction has been clear to those who grasped the broader context. The term 'Revolution in Military Affairs', coined at that time, captured the magnitude of the change, even if it failed to express its root cause: the electronic revolution. And since then, the revolution and its transformational effect on warfare have only deepened.

Let us focus on the tank, a product of the second, mechanization revolution and the backbone of land warfare for about 100 years. Ever since World War II, tanks have been optimized primarily to fight other tanks and, second, to withstand hollow charges. Their main armament is a high-velocity gun firing kinetic projectiles. In most armies, half of their 60–70-ton weight consists of heavy armor, which in turn requires a 1,500 horsepower engine. However, tanks will no longer come within kinetic firing range of each other. They will be discovered and attacked at much longer ranges. This is no different than what happened to the mighty battleships of World War II's Pacific theater, which never came within firing range of each other. The adjustment of the tank's gun to launch guided missiles bypasses the question of what the current utility of the heavy kinetic gun itself is. The tank's heavy armor has similarly reached the limits of its ability to withstand precision, tandem hollow-charge, fire-and-forget munitions, which target the tank's vulnerable top. The wholesale destruction of the hapless Armenian army in the 2020 war against Azerbaijan, like the stranded and harassed Russian convoy en route to Kiev and the iconic image of a Russian armored battalion massacred during its attempted river crossing in the Donbas, with a shattered bridge in the middle, starkly demonstrates the current reality.

This does not mean that the tank and other fighting vehicles are history. But the answer may not be found in further reinforcing the heavy armor or in improved tactical practices, clumsy as Russian tactics proved to be. Rather, the answer seems to lie in a full-scale adjustment of land fighting vehicles to the ongoing electronic revolution. Above all, this means the adoption of active defense systems, such as the Israeli Trophy and Iron Fist, purchased by the US, German, and British armies. Active defense includes electronic detection, disruption, and interception of incoming projectiles, launched from land or from the air—the same revolution that sea and air warfare have already undergone. Electronic systems designed to disrupt and down unmanned aerial vehicles attacking either individually or in swarms are similarly being developed and introduced. As such systems will become standard everywhere, they will transform land warfare. The current reality, in which being detected on the modern battlefield means almost assured destruction, will no longer hold. A two-sided game reopens. Battlefield survival and success will depend on the question of which side possesses the last word in terms of offensive and defensive electronic systems and counter-systems for detection, attack, interception, and disruption.

The modern tanks and infantry fighting vehicles supplied to Ukraine by the West lack active defense systems. Despite their heavy armor and great sophistication, they seem to be almost as vulnerable to modern electronically guided munitions as the Russian models have been. The World War I style trench warfare stalemate that has attracted so much attention may be a function of this current imbalance between defensive and offensive arms. Moreover, active defense systems are presently installed on heavily armored fighting vehicles as something *extra*, whereas they are in fact destined to *replace* the heavy armor, whose effectiveness has in any case plummeted. This makes current armored fighting vehicles installed with active defense systems intermediate breeds that combine two eras—the old and the new. The heavy armor is no more necessary for land fighting vehicles than the 350–400mm steel armor of the past is necessary for warships today. It is a *disadvantage*. Relying on electronic detection and interception systems enables a drastic reduction in the armor of fighting vehicles for what is necessary against small arms, shrapnel, and blasts. Thus, there is expected to be a great reduction in their weight, a parallel reduction in their engine size, and a design re-orientation to electronically guided defensive and offensive systems. To this, connectivity, automation, and cyber—defensive and offensive alike—are added. That, I suggest, is the direction in which land warfare and land fighting vehicles are heading in the electronic-computerized age.

This projected foray into the future is just an example intended to illustrate the continuous challenge posed by successive technological waves that have transformed the conduct of war since the onset of the industrial-technological age at the beginning of the nineteenth century. Each of these technological revolutions has given birth to its own highly elaborate doctrines as to how armed forces should be built, equipped, and fight. Without minimizing the significance of universal precepts embedded in the nature of war, it is these history-dependent doctrines, and their practical application in terms of investment, organization, and training, that constitute the main stuff of military theory.

Let us now turn to two forms of irregular warfare—guerrilla and terrorism—that have increasingly captured the headlines since the late nineteenth century and are often viewed as fundamental 'categories'. We examine how they have sweepingly changed—sometimes at their very 'core'—with historical transformation.

How Has Guerrilla Become a Recipe for Success?

Guerrilla warfare is as old as regular state armies. What defines it is the eschewing of direct confrontation in the open field against a superior enemy in favor of hit-and-run action against isolated detachments and outposts, attacks on supplies, and other indirect means. Generally, it is the weapon of the weak, and it aims to win by attrition.

While it has been practiced throughout history, guerrilla warfare has reached an entirely new level of success over the past century. It has earned a reputation of near invincibility, driving great powers out of their former colonial empires and frustrating military interventions even where the asymmetry in force capability has been the starkest. Why have mighty powers that proved capable of crushing the strongest of opponents failed to defeat the humblest of military rivals in some of the world's poorest and weakest regions? This is the puzzle of guerrilla: how do the weak defeat the strong? It is supposed to be the opposite. The puzzle is even greater because the guerrilla's image of near invincibility stands in sharp contrast to its often low military effectiveness. Insurgents have rarely been able to defeat regular armies militarily, and they sustain far greater losses than they inflict, sometimes to a crippling degree.

Nearly all the attempts to explain the puzzle have emphasized some supposedly general/universal features of guerrilla. Thus, it has been suggested that the problem of counterinsurgency lies in the number of troops and resources that a great power can spare for a particular local war, given its overall commitments and the difficulties of power projection to faraway theaters.[9] Another argument advanced to the effect of the asymmetry in strength between the sides being less stark than meets the eye is that other great powers sometimes support and arm the guerrillas. Such, for example, was the case with the Soviet support of North Vietnam and the Vietcong, and with the United States' aid to the Mujahedeen in Afghanistan against the Soviet Union during the 1980s. In many other cases, however, external support did not play a significant role in the guerrillas' success. According to yet another explanation, the developed powers have a lower interest and, hence, lesser motivation in the conflict than those of indigenous forces. Thus, the 'balance of resolve' supposedly outweighs the 'balance of capabilities' in such unequal wars.[10]

Although these attempted explanations for the puzzle of guerrilla clearly have some validity, each and all of them together still do not seem to account for the sweeping scale and magnitude of guerrilla warfare's chain of successes since the beginning of the twentieth century. Moreover, none of these general explanations give any clue as to why the effectiveness of guerrilla warfare has suddenly skyrocketed during this period. What has *changed*? Rather than being grounded in some fundamental feature of guerrilla warfare, the puzzle seems to be more time-bound and condition-dependent. Indeed, my friend Gil Merom has pointed to the obvious explanation: rather than being universal, the difficulty with fighting guerrilla has overwhelmingly been the lot of liberal democratic powers—and encountered precisely because they are liberal democratic. While everyone seems to know this answer in some corner of their mind, it is still far from being generally recognized by scholars and in the public discussion at large.

Throughout history, argues Merom, imperial 'pacification' rested on the overt threat and actual application of ruthless violence to crush resistance in subject societies. Where the people offered insurgents support and sympathy, they became exposed to sweeping reprisals by the ruling power, including killing, looting, burning, enslavement, and mass deportations. The *ultima ratio* of imperial control was the threat of genocide. All empires worked this way, including democratic and republican ones, such as ancient Athens and Rome. They could *only* work this way. Much the same applies to the conduct of present-day nondemocratic powers. However, sometime towards the end of the nineteenth century, the conduct that has sustained empires throughout history became increasingly unacceptable in emergent liberal democratic societies.[11]

Britain, the world's largest empire and most liberal country, best typifies the trend. In the Boer War in South Africa (1899–1902), Britain initially suffered humiliating defeats in regular fighting. When half a million British troops were dispatched to South Africa, regular Boer resistance was crushed, only to give way to widespread irregular resistance. Unable to suppress that resistance, the British resorted to pretty draconic measures, rounding up the Boer civilian population into concentration camps. (The term originates from this period, long before it would assume its horrendous meaning later in the century.) Owing to the poor hygienic–sanitary conditions of the time, some 30,000 people perished there from various diseases. And yet Britain was able to declare victory only by offering the Boers the most generous of peace terms that within a few years effectively surrendered to them governmental powers over all of the newly created South African Federation.

Far more telling than the war in South Africa was Ireland, which was an integral part of the United Kingdom rather than a far-away colony. In the late nineteenth and early twentieth centuries, the Irish resumed their quest for independence from the United Kingdom, and their struggle was crowned with success. How did the Irish, whose periodic rebellions over the centuries had been repeatedly drowned in blood, suddenly succeed in seceding? It was only when the demand for self-determination became hard to resist by liberals, who also found the old methods of forceful suppression repugnant and unacceptable that Ireland was able to gain independence. For although British counterinsurgency tactics proved quite effective in 1919–1921, they could never completely quell the rebellion, given the restriction on ruthlessness towards civilians under which British forces operated. Indeed, South Africa and Ireland were the signs of things to come in liberal countries' counterinsurgency wars.

Since the Vietnam War, the liberal democracies' record of failure in fighting guerrillas has often been attributed to the effects of television coverage. It should be noted, however, that Britain lost the struggle against Irish independence long before television, as was effectively the case with the loss of its empire in general. Similarly, the French lost the war in Vietnam (1946–1954) before the advent of television that would allegedly lose the war for the Americans in the same theater. Even the French loss of the war in Algeria (1954–1962) effectively predated the age of television coverage. The transmission of the horrors and atrocities of war into American living rooms through television only reinforced a trend which had already been strongly evident before television.[12]

It has also been argued that democratic countries tend to lose wars against irregulars because of the democracies' inability to withstand protracted wars of attrition.[13] However, in both world wars, grinding attrition was actually the democracies' strategy of choice, whereas their rivals,

Germany and Japan, sought rapid decision by lightning campaigns. In the Cold War, too, it was the liberal democracies that outlasted the Soviets in the protracted conflict of materiel and endurance. Furthermore, eight years of war for the French in Algeria, eight for the Americans in Vietnam and twenty in Afghanistan hardly constitute short struggles. It was the futility of these wars given the democracies' self-imposed restrictions on brutality that accounted for their length and ultimately led to the democracies' withdrawal. Conversely, the brutality of authoritarian regimes often cuts insurgencies short.

Do not get this wrong. The liberal democracies' conduct against guerrillas during the twentieth and twenty-first centuries has been far from saintly. They have still wielded formidable instruments of coercion and pressure, and their conduct has often been quite brutal. Civilians are killed and atrocities are sometimes committed, occurring either with the authorities turning a blind eye or on the troops' own initiative. All the same, strict restrictions on the use of violence against civilians constitute the legal and normative standard for liberal democracies. And although many, probably most, violations of this standard remain unreported, numerous incidents have been exposed in open societies with free media and are met with public condemnation and judicial procedures. All these radically limit the liberal democracies' powers of suppression, judged by historical and comparative standards.

Some have suggested that democracies have been at least as inclined as non-democracies to target civilians, if not more so. The British starvation blockade of Germany in World War I and Allied city bombing campaigns against Germany and Japan in World War II are major examples.[14] However, such instances predominantly occurred in desperate major wars for survival—a category that excludes the overwhelming majority of counterinsurgency wars against weak non-state rivals. Indeed, the more intense the threat, the more likely are the democracies to relax their restrictions on the targeting of civilians in counterinsurgency operations as well.

It is not that the 'balance of resolve' versus the 'balance of capabilities' does not matter in accounting for the failure of counterinsurgency. True, Ireland was not a far-away colony but had been an integral part of the United Kingdom for centuries. Algeria, too, was regarded by the French as part of metropolitan France. The possibility of retreat tore France apart and brought it to the brink of civil war, not least because it involved the uprooting and removal of millions of European settlers who had lived in Algeria for generations. Still, the locals' resolve to win independence in both Ireland and Algeria was stronger. More telling is Israel's case with respect to the territories occupied in 1967, which constitute the core of the country historically and strategically. Confronting the same problems in fighting insurgents as all other liberal democracies, Israel found it necessary to withdraw from much of these Palestinian-inhabited territories in the mid-1990s and in 2005, in the wake of the first and second Palestinian Intifadas or uprisings. However, once it occurred to Israelis that the aims of Palestinian fighting were more radical than the establishment of an independent state in these territories alongside Israel—that they did not give up on their dream of eliminating Israel—things changed. Israel was able to mobilize its forces, successfully re-occupy the West Bank from 2002 on, and militarily crush the Second Intifada, which did not mean the end of the century-long conflict, of course.

Indeed, as this book was being completed, Hamas' October 7th 2023 surprise attack from the Gaza Strip, which slaughtered some 1,200 Israeli civilians, has brought about a full-scale Israeli offensive to crush Hamas. This is something that Israel had tried to avoid for two decades, inter alia because of the inevitable civilian casualties and destruction in Gaza that such a step was certain to cause. Hamas has purposefully nestled itself within, and literally dug itself in a labyrinth of tunnels deep into, the Palestinian population in densely urban areas in the hopes of gaining immunity from attack. Moreover, Hamas used the civilian environment to launch thousands of rockets against Israel's cities and towns—an unprecedented situation, as guerrilla warfare has so far taken place continents and oceans away from the state the guerrillas were fighting. Given Hamas' deep interweaving into the civilian environment, destruction in

Gaza has been massive and civilian death and suffering very significant indeed. Still, anyone who claims that the killing and destruction in Gaza is unacceptable should provide other practical and convincing methods that would break Hamas's power. Otherwise, they are effectively arguing that Hamas should have immunity from attack. Many critics have evaded this question, and some seem to be effectively in favor of granting Hamas such immunity under the circumstances.

In his *Just and Unjust Wars* (1977), philosopher Michael Walzer has coined the concept 'supreme emergency' to describe exceptional circumstances that justified extraordinary ruthlessness, such as that of the Allies' bombing campaign in their life-and-death struggle with the Axis powers. Even under such circumstances for Israel's war in Gaza, its armed forces have targeted only places from which Hamas carries out the war, which unfortunately consist of most of the urban environment, above and below the ground. They have also taken every step to evacuate the civilian population from the areas of military operations. Legal advisers throughout the chain of command are entrusted with authorizing all the military measures taken. For these reasons, the ratio of civilians to armed men killed—estimated at 1.5 civilians to 1 armed man—remains much lower than that recorded by the US forces in their recent counterinsurgency campaigns, to say nothing of the conduct of non-democratic states in similar circumstances.

Indeed, totalitarian and authoritarian regimes constitute our control group. For if the argument presented here is valid, then nondemocratic powers ought to exhibit a substantially better record of success in curbing insurgency by ruthless means. In assessing this, a widely overlooked problem clouds our vision. Sherlock Holmes called it 'the curious case of the dog that didn't bark'. We only notice the dogs that bark. In more professional jargon, there is a serious selection bias involved. Guerrilla warfare against the colonial powers typically took place against Western democracies, which turned all the attention to them. However, although authoritarian and totalitarian great powers in the twentieth century also possessed empires, none of them were broken up by guerrilla wars of national liberation, which had practically no chance of success in their cases.[15] The empires of both Imperial and Nazi Germany, as well as that of Imperial Japan, were eliminated by the victors in the two world wars. The Soviet empire, both inside the Soviet Union itself and in Eastern Europe, fell apart, and its many peoples broke loose only after the Soviet totalitarian system had been dismantled. As long as the totalitarian system was in place, everybody within these empires knew all too well what fate awaited those that would dare to revolt. Indeed, they were brutally crushed if they tried.

Cases of authoritarian and totalitarian suppression merit close attention. Countless atrocities were performed in colonial settings by all imperial powers, irrespective of their regimes.[16] And yet, even by the European colonial standards in Africa, Imperial Germany's conduct was exceptional. In German Southwest Africa, today's Namibia, the Herero revolt in 1904 was countered by a policy and strategy of extermination. Wells were sealed off, and much of the population was driven out to the desert to die, while the others were worked to death in labor camps. Only 15,000 out of 80,000 Herero survived. In German East Africa, today's Tanzania, the Maji–Maji revolt in 1905–1907 was similarly answered with extermination. A small force of 500 German troops destroyed settlements and crops so systematically that more than a quarter of a million natives died, mostly of starvation.[17] These were chilling demonstrations of the effectiveness of the old techniques of imperial suppression, which ultimately rested on the threat and practice of genocide.

Imperial Japan was able to subdue Taiwan (occupied in 1895), Korea (1905), and Manchuria (1931), as it very likely would have been able to accomplish throughout its 'East Asian Co-Prosperity Sphere' had its empire survived World War II. There are no indications that indigenous resistance would have stood a chance of succeeding against the authoritarian-totalitarian great powers. These powers were less involved in imperial wars of suppression precisely because they were so effective in suppression that resistance was not allowed to grow into insurgency and was deterred before it flared up. As Sherlock Holmes noted, it is the countries and people held down under the totalitarian iron fist that are the most conspicuous.

Sceptiks might argue that despite Nazi Germany's unbridled use of terror to secure total compliance in the countries of occupied Europe, it failed to suppress guerrillas in occupied parts of both the Soviet Union and Yugoslavia. However, there can be little doubt that had Germany won the war and been able to redirect more forces to these troublesome spots from her overstretched fronts, her genocidal methods would have also prevailed there.

Critics might further argue that the Soviet Union failed in Afghanistan (1979–1988) despite the Soviets' brutal tactics. However, ruthlessness has always been a *necessary* but not *sufficient* condition for effective suppression. Afghanistan—vast, desolate, and sparsely populated—historically the ideal guerrilla country, was actually the *exception*, the *outlier*, in the vast Soviet imperial system. This system remained unbroken for many decades under the Soviet iron fist, including countries with a justified reputation of fierce nationalism such as Poland and Hungary. Chechnya is a more telling example than Afghanistan: under Stalin, the Soviet Union harbored no scruples in deporting entire populations, including the Chechens, *en masse* from their homeland. By contrast, liberalizing Russia of the 1990s was forced to give in to Chechen insurgents, whereas the Russia that has been turning in a more authoritarian direction under Putin proved tenacious in crushing this resistance by ruthless means. The order on the scale of brutality and effectiveness is unmistakable. It is no coincidence that the disintegration of the empire and the secession of the former Soviet republics took place only after the breakdown of the Soviet system, rather than at any time before.

Gandhi became an iconic figure for advocating and successfully practicing the doctrine of non-violent resistance against British rule in India. With the rise of Hitlerism and the outbreak of World War II, he advised the Jews to opt for mass disobedience against Nazi genocidal persecution. He later called on the peoples of Europe as well, including Britain, to embrace civil defiance against a German invasion, in preference over armed resistance, so as to 'shame' Nazi Germany away from its prey.[18] This fatuous universalization of his famed doctrine only highlighted the unique historical and political conditions within which it was able to work, and succeed: that is, solely when directed against a liberal democratic power. It was India's good fortune to have struggled for independence against liberal Britain. Had India been ruled by Imperial Japan, Nazi Germany, or the Soviet Union, Mr Gandhi, as he was invariably referred to politely by the British authorities and media, would have disappeared after first raising his voice, and nobody would have known who he was.

All the above is surely not a recommendation for democracies to adopt the old ways of wholesale suppression and indiscriminate killing. It does, however, put things into the correct perspective. The much-belabored formula in the West that the way to win counterinsurgency war is by 'winning the hearts and minds' of the population has yielded poor results. In most cases, this goal is almost impossible to achieve in foreign countries whose populations usually identify more with their insurgent compatriots. In addition, 'winning the hearts and minds' tends to be extremely expensive compared to the terrifyingly low costs of ruthless suppression. The United States' withdrawal from Afghanistan, after it spent trillions of dollars on both military occupation and huge hopeful and hopeless civil projects over twenty years, is the most recent tell-tale demonstration of this sad reality.

The increasing use of urban environment by insurgents is another recent demonstration of liberal democracies' self-imposed limitations. Historically, insurgency flourished mostly in the remote parts of the countryside: deserts, mountains, forests, and swamps. Urban environment constitutes a deadly trap against an enemy who has no scruples about indiscriminately felling buildings and setting cities on fire, as in the past, or razing them to the ground with artillery fire, as in modern times. However, more recently, irregulars fighting against liberal democratic powers have been moving to the cities and making them their bastions precisely because they have been able to take shelter within the urban-civilian environment, while relying on their opponents to refrain from operating indiscriminately in these settings.

Compare this to the conduct of President Hafez al-Assad of Syria, who in 1982 had whole neighborhoods in the city of Hama destroyed with artillery fire, when his army brutally suppressed a revolt by the Muslim Brotherhood, killing an estimated 10,000–25,000 of the city's population in three days. The Muslim Brotherhood was crushed so severely that they remained ineffective for nearly twenty years afterward.

Putin's Russia was as successful in suppressing the ferocious Chechen resistance (1999–2000), using similar methods and destroying large parts of Chechnya's capital city, Grozny. Indeed, the Russian intervention in the Syrian civil war in 2015 secured victory for the Bashar al-Assad regime which had been on the verge of defeat. The Russian force in Syria comprised just over thirty aircraft. By comparison, the United States has had some ten times the number of aircraft in the Middle East, and the Israeli Air Force is also roughly ten times larger than the Russian contingent in Syria was. Both the American and Israeli air forces are also several times more sophisticated technologically and tactically than the Russian air force, as the war in Ukraine amply demonstrated. And yet, neither the United States nor Israel have been able to achieve anything even remotely commensurable with the Russian victory in Syria in their own counterinsurgency campaigns: in Afghanistan, Iraq, and Syria, for the United States, and against Hezbollah in Southern Lebanon and Hamas in Gaza, for Israel, over twenty years—at least until the recent spate of war in Gaza and Lebanon. The reason for this stark difference is obvious: the Russians had no scruples about indiscriminately destroying the city of Aleppo, one of the Syrian insurgents' major strongholds, systematically felling the buildings on the heads of both the insurgents and civilian population. Thereafter, this example and the impending threat of further such actions were sufficient to bring about the surrender of the other rebel strongholds in Syria.

Thus, in contrast to the democracies, authoritarian and totalitarian powers have crushed any resistance in their domain with an iron fist, as they continue to do. From this perspective, a Uighur or Tibetan insurgency against China has very few prospects of success as long as China's regime remains. This is not to say that democracies *always* lose counterinsurgency wars, while non-democracies *always* win. But the balance is sharply tilted against the democracies in such struggles.

The democracies' evolving response to this reality has factored in both their weaknesses and strengths. Above all, they try to avoid foreign entanglements whenever possible. When intervention against serious security threats becomes unavoidable, they seek to refrain from placing 'boots on the ground' as much as possible. Instead, they tend to adopt two other lines of action. First, they look for indigenous allies, which not only enjoy greater local legitimacy than a foreign power and are more familiar with the local populations but are also less constrained in carrying out the 'dirty work' of land warfare and occupation. Examples include: the Northern Alliance during the American conquest of Afghanistan; the Sunni tribal leaders whose cooperation was the main reason for the weakening of al-Qaeda in Iraq during the 'Surge'; the Kurds in the fight against ISIS in both Iraq and Syria; the South Lebanese Army which Israel cultivated before its withdrawal from Lebanon in 2000; and the security forces of the Palestinian Authority in the West Bank. Although not all these surrogate forces have been equally successful, they are among the democracies' few remaining viable options.

Second, the United States and Israel are the world leaders in adapting high-tech warfare to the task of fighting irregulars. They have been increasingly investing in surveillance, tracking, and targeting electronic and robotic systems, designed to dig out low-signature irregulars operating in a dense civilian environment. The limitations of all these measures, as compared to ruthless suppression, have often been demonstrated. But, again, they are the best that the democracies have to offer at this stage in the development of guerrilla and counter-guerrilla warfare.

To conclude, rather than being a function of guerrilla warfare's intrinsic features, as most of the literature on the subject assumes, guerrilla's remarkable record of success during the last 100 years turns out to be almost entirely the result of a very particular, yet crucial, factor: the liberal democracies' self-imposed restraints. Not that they get much credit for this by either friend or foe, partly because the reasons for the success of guerrilla warfare have not been recognized for what they are—arising in fact from the democracies' noblest of traits.

Terrorism: Eternal or New? And Where Is It Heading?

What exactly is meant by terrorism is notoriously ambiguous. One reason for this is the mixing of normative and functional elements in the discussion. 'One man's terrorist is another man's freedom fighter' is a well-known pronouncement. It reflect the normative tension between state authorities' derogatory use of the term, seeking to outcast terrorism, and the opposite view that terrorism may be morally justified, heroic, and noble in fighting oppression. Thus, most of us would probably support terrorist action against Nazism (how successful it could be is another matter); many thought the same about terrorism in the service of a struggle against colonial rule; and around 1900, some thought so about terrorist action against the 'oppressive' capitalist system. The normative distinction between all such cases is value-dependent. To this should be added another difference that is regarded as morally significant: terrorists attack civilian targets intentionally—this element of the definition is widely shared. However, whereas some terrorist groups target government or 'establishment' institutions, offices, and individuals, others target civilian populations indiscriminately and randomly. States, too, might target civilians intentionally (the unintended killing of civilians in military operations is ubiquitous), and in this sense one might reasonably talk about state terrorism. But, for our purposes, we shall leave this, as well as any normative perspective, aside, and settle on the following rough definition as best reflecting the most common use of what people mean by terrorism: the attack on civilian targets by small groups or individuals for political purposes.

Terrorist attacks, such as the assassination of the Austrian Crown Prince Franz Ferdinand in July 1914 and the 9/11 terror attack on the United States, have sometimes led to wars. But should terrorism itself be considered a warlike activity and be discussed in a book such as this one? Again, this question involves more than semantic distinctions between war and other forms of lethal violence; contrary to a prevailing view, rather than existing from time immemorial, terrorism in the sense described emerged quite recently, from the late nineteenth century onward. Moreover, it might be evolving into something of an entirely new scale and magnitude as we move into the twenty-first century.

Although terrorism is widely claimed to have existed throughout history, only the assassination of leaders is as old as humanity.[19] It was not before the final decades of the nineteenth century, on the heels of modern technological and social developments, that individuals and small groups acquired the ability to kill a substantial number of people before they realized what was happening and could respond by fight or flight. The same applied to the newly acquired, much enhanced ability to bring down buildings and other installations. We begin with weapon technologies. The revolver from the late nineteenth century, the submachine gun from World War I onward, and the assault rifle (such as the iconic AK-47 Kalashnikov) from after World War II have increasingly made surprise, extensive killing possible. The invention of high explosives in the 1880s, replacing black powder after its thousand-year reign, had a similar effect on both people and infrastructure. Indeed, the 'terrorists of dynamite' and those of the revolver inaugurated terrorism as a major public phenomenon in both Tsarist Russia and throughout the West from the 1880s onward.

The simultaneous developments in communication technology have also been crucial. Trains, followed by cars and, from the 1960s on, passenger jets, have made mobility across countries and later continents a reality not only for the masses who had previously not left their native villages, but also for terrorists. It was now a matter of hours or days to reach the provincial or country capital and seat of government. A no less sweeping revolution took place in the communication of information. Popular newspapers, fed with national and world news by telegraph networks that spread across countries and, from the last third of the nineteenth century, crossed oceans, made terrorist actions household events. Radio and television would reinforce the trend during the twentieth century. Terrorism has been aptly described as a public relations act. In the grand scheme of things, both the actual number of those killed and the material damage done by terrorist attacks are minuscule. As the name suggests, the real effect is achieved through psychological terror. Terrorism lives on in its resonance in the media and among the public. Without that resonance, like the proverbial falling tree in a forest where nobody is present and listening, terrorist acts make no sound and are inconsequential.

Before proceeding from when terrorism emerged to where it is heading, a few comments are in order on how successful it has been and against whom. By and large, terrorism has had a chance of succeeding only against democracies and weak authoritarian regimes. Its prospects of success against strong authoritarian, let alone totalitarian, regimes are practically nil. The reasons for this are clear enough. First, totalitarian and strong authoritarian regimes' penetration of society, social control, policing, and lack of legal constraints nip potential terrorist organizations in the bud. Second, these regimes deny terrorists the media coverage on which they thrive. In line with the first principle of public relations, terrorism that is not reported has no noticeable effect. By contrast, democracies are most vulnerable to terrorism because of both their legal constraints and the massive media coverage the phenomenon receives in open societies. Acts of terrorism in such countries ring every bell.

That said, terrorist successes against democracies have been very uneven. From the outset, terrorism has been employed in the service of two main causes: social revolution, mostly by anarchists and socialists, and national liberation. Jihadist terrorism also emerged and has moved to the forefront from the late twentieth century onward—both in its home countries and internationally. Generally, terrorists of national liberation—building on liberal sensitivities and the principle of national self-definition—have been quite successful, not always and everywhere, but still in a very wide range of cases. By contrast, terrorists of social revolution have invariably failed: from those active throughout the West around 1900 to the likes of Baader-Meinhof in Germany, the Red Brigades in Italy, and the Red Army in Japan, all springing up in the 1970s. Their demand for a total restructuring of society was too far-reaching to be acceptable. And, indeed, unlike the terrorists of national liberation, they lacked broad public support among their populations. Isolated, they were ultimately hunted down by the police. Also of the social breed but coming from the opposite direction, there has been an emergence of far-right, mostly lone actor, terrorism in the United States and elsewhere since the 1990s. It has been fed by extreme anarchist-libertarian, religious fundamentalist, white supremacist, anti-immigration, or anti-Muslim persuasions. Islamist-Jihadist terrorism has rocked the world in many ways, but its concrete record of successes has thus far been very ambiguous.

For all that, there is more to fear than fear itself. In recent decades, terrorism has thrived on both high-tech and low-tech technologies. The revolution in communication technology thanks to the internet has magnified access to information concerning methods and means, as well as the spread of propaganda. It has given rise to burgeoning 'franchise subsidiaries' of the leading terrorist brands. Widely available electronic gadgets such as cellphones and, around the corner, drones and robots, are some of the new high-tech devices that fuse with the low-tech homing method of suicide bombing. Of the latter variety, we now have human-guided aircraft, human-guided lorries, and human walking bombs. However, by far the greatest threat is the prospect of unconventional terrorism using weapons of mass destruction (WMD).

Unconventional weapons or WMD are an assortment of unconnected technologies with widely diverging potency. Their only common denominator is that they are prohibited by international law. The potential use of chemical weapons by terrorists is predicated on the element of surprise, catching concentrated crowds of people unawares and unprotected and therefore highly vulnerable. However, chemical weapons pose the least serious threat of the WMDs, because of the high volume of chemical agents needed and the problem of spreading them effectively and undetected with the means terrorists might possess. A highly successful chemical terror attack is estimated to have a casualty potential in the thousands.

Nuclear weapons stand at the opposite pole. Not only is their destructive power horrendous, but there is also no effective defense against them that is even remotely commensurate with their destructiveness. In the absence of effective defense, mutual deterrence has become the dominant strategic rationale among nuclear powers and has prevented a nuclear war—and arguably any war—between them since 1945. Herein lies the bewildering danger of the new unconventional terror: deterrence is infinitely less effective against terrorist groups than it is against states. Not only are such groups more likely to consist of extremist zealots willing to sacrifice their own lives and even positively desiring a general apocalypse; they are also too elusive to offer a clear enough target for retaliation, on which the whole concept of deterrence is based.

Terrorists cannot produce fissile material by themselves, at least not in the foreseeable future. However, tests carried out by scientists for the American authorities suggest that a primitive nuclear bomb can be built from parts available on the open market, with fissile material that is bought or stolen. Nuclear know-how or even the weapons themselves might be stolen or bought on the black market, and apparently not very expensively. Abdul Qadeer Khan, the Pakistani nuclear scientist who headed his country's program to manufacture an atomic bomb, sold nuclear secrets to perhaps a dozen countries—from Southeast Asia to the Middle East, including North Korea, Iran, and Libya—reportedly for as little as millions or tens of millions of dollars. Indeed, the danger of leakage of nuclear materials, expertise, or even the weapons themselves may be the greatest in less developed countries. In many of them, security standards are low, state authority is weak, corruption is widespread, and organized crime thrives. Some of these countries are in danger of disintegration and anarchy. If this happens, say in Pakistan, who will guarantee the security of a country's nuclear arsenal? The collapsed Soviet Union, with its scattered nuclear facilities and unemployed nuclear scientists—the cause of much concern during the 1990s—may be the model for future threats more than the former nuclear superpower.

However, perhaps the greatest threat comes from biological weapons, which combine potentially massive lethality that brings them close to nuclear weapons with much greater accessibility. This has become increasingly recognized from about 2000 on, long before the outbreak of the coronavirus pandemic. Throughout history, big epidemics were much greater killers than wars, with a virulent strain of influenza killing an estimated twenty to forty million people worldwide in 1918–1919, more than had died in World War I. Since then, medicine has largely subdued infectious diseases. However, the revolutionary breakthroughs in decoding the genome and genetic engineering during recent decades have massively magnified the threat of biological terrorism. Biotechnology is one of the spearheads of today's technological revolution. As a result, processes that were impossible only a generation ago, or required heavy state infrastructure and great expense, can now be carried out cheaply by thousands of laboratories around the world.[20] The products of this revolution might be devastating. According to a Congressional assessment made as early as 1993, a light plane flying over Washington D.C. and spraying 100 kilograms of military-quality anthrax could kill three million people.

Thus, the great new threat facing humanity is the trickling down of the technologies and materials of WMD to below the state level. For much of history, non-state players such as tribal and armed gang leaders challenged states successfully. With modernity, states' dominance increased as they increasingly controlled the heavy infrastructure underlying military power. Although states still dominate, despite encroachments from various directions, the encapsulation of destructive power in WMD, particularly nuclear but also biological, recreates a situation in which a player no longer needs to be big in order to deliver a devastating punch. Indeed, even though states possess far greater unconventional capability than terrorists, the latter are *more* likely than states to use the ultimate weapons. In contrast to the habits of mind that have dominated since the onset of the nuclear age, unconventional capabilities acquired by terrorists are *usable*. World-threatening individuals and organizations, previously the preserve of James Bond-style fiction, have suddenly become real.

Seeking out such agents of destruction in vast and largely inaccessible tracts of the globe inhabited by fragmented and unruly societies may be harder than finding a needle in a haystack. Developed countries as well might be very difficult to monitor effectively. The Aum Shinrikyo cult in Japan, which carried out the first (very primitive) terrorist chemical attack in the Tokyo subway in 1995, built its facilities for the manufacture of biological and chemical agents undetected in one of the world's most advanced countries. The perpetrators of the September 11, 2001 conventional mega-terror attacks trained in Germany and the United States. In separate incidents in 2003, British and French police raided residences where Islamic extremists were preparing ricin and botulinum toxins from chemical materials ordered on the open market. The notion of 'a bomb in the basement', originally conceived in relation to states' undeclared development of nuclear weapons, has acquired a chilling new meaning. And once the potential exists, it is difficult to see what will stop it from being realized by someone, somewhere.

It has been found that people in the West vastly exaggerate the threat of conventional terrorism. More people died in the months after 9/11 by switching from air flight to accident-prone cars than in the terror attack itself. More people die in the United States every year by falling from ladders or drowning in their own bathtubs than by terrorist acts. Still, in public opinion polls, people place terrorism very high as a probable cause of death, whereas in reality the prospect of such a death is minuscule. However, with unconventional terrorism, the picture changes radically. Biological or nuclear terrorism may cause a disaster on par with the United States' most severe wars, while the means for preventing this form of terrorism do not seem promising.[21]

Cyber terrorism is another emerging threat. The virtual anonymity of cyber attacks under present conditions makes it difficult to distinguish between those conducted by state or state-sponsored actors and those conducted by non-state or terrorist groups. For all that, state and state-sponsored cyber attacks are difficult to conceal for long, with the result that mutual deterrence between states regarding massive cyber attacks still holds to a very considerable degree. By contrast, here too cyber attacks by terrorist groups are far more difficult to deter. How much computing power such groups will be able to master, how vulnerable their targets will prove to be, and how lethal, destructive, and disruptive such terrorist cyber attacks might become is something that only the future will tell.

To conclude, we have seen the deep historicity of both guerrilla warfare and terrorism: their specific time of emergence on the heels of modern technological and social developments (terrorism); their widely varying efficacy against democratic and nondemocratic rivals (both guerrilla and terrorism); and their potentially massive transformation with the adoption of new technological breakthroughs that might revolutionize their very 'core' (terrorism, but also guerrilla). Terrorism may be on the verge of a change that might make it one of the greatest security—indeed, military—challenges of the future. From a primarily public relations activity that it has been since its inception in the 1880s, terrorism could become the perpetrator of mass killing, unconstrained by mutual deterrence that is close to being the only defense against weapons of mass destruction.

The Ultimate Weapon

The most significant technological breakthrough affecting war has been the advent of nuclear weapons. They constitute a class of their own that sets them apart from all other known weapons. Not only is their destructive power so great that a large enough nuclear stockpile can destroy any rival, indeed, the whole of humanity; there is also no effective defense against them that is even remotely commensurable with their destructiveness. Their overwhelming destructive power is not offset by any equal rise in defensive power, as has been the case with many other military technologies.

It is these qualities that make nuclear weapons the first ultimate weapon, which leaves no doubt as to the result of their wholesale use and nullifies any hope of gain in a war in which they are massively employed by both sides. It may sound strange at first, but for war to occur, *both* sides need to choose it, assessing it to be preferable to the alternatives, including surrender. One of the sides, sometimes both, is likely to be wrong in its assessment of the outcome of the war. But it is the uncertainty, the information gap, with respect to the future, that leaves space for the sides to take their chances, and gives rise to war. This uncertainty, a crucial element of the nature of war in the sense described, was to contract to near zero with the quantum leap represented by the advent of the ultimate weapon, as destructive power swung to the very extreme.

During the first fifteen years of the nuclear age, until about 1960, the two nuclear superpowers—the United States and the Soviet Union—still believed in, and diligently prepared for, victory in a nuclear war between them. The number of nuclear bombs was still relatively limited, and their delivery by bomber aircraft was still hazardous, leaving room for uncertainty regarding the outcome of such a war, highly destructive as it was expected to be. However, with the coming of nuclear abundance and missile delivery systems, the uncertainty was all but eliminated, and any illusion regarding the outcome evaporated. By the early 1960s, the notion of mutual assured destruction (MAD) in case of a superpowers' nuclear war had sunk in and become the prevailing doctrine. Despite persistent fears of a 'first strike' by the other side, both knew for certain that they could only lose in an all-out nuclear war. In the absence of any effective defence against nuclear weapons, deterrence—which had always been central to conflict, human as in nature at large—now came to the fore and became the central pillar of nuclear strategy. It is widely credited for preventing a nuclear war and arguably any war between nuclear countries so far.

Nuclear strategy has thus evolved from its initial stage of preparing for Armageddon to the later prevalence of MAD between the nuclear superpowers, now including China. Furthermore, the logic of MAD seems to hold also for lesser nuclear countries, such as India, Pakistan, North Korea, and potentially others in the future, even when the asymmetry in nuclear power is the greatest (as, for example, between the United States and North Korea). Nuclear weapons have long been called the 'great equalizer' for this reason (though this does not apply to other dimensions of power). All the same, although the logic of MAD is so overwhelming that it is widely seen as inviolable, it would be a mistake to regard it as absolute. Thinking about nuclear weapons has been shaped by the Cold War clash of titans between the United

States and the Soviet Union. But it is the minnows that might stretch the logic of MAD.

Certainly, the major nuclear powers continue to dominate in all respects, and the logic of MAD remains extremely compelling. At the same time, the taboo against both the use and threat of use of nuclear weapons, which has taken root since the 1960s and has been extended to non-nuclear powers as well, not protected by the logic of MAD, has been eroding before our eyes. As these lines are being written, Russia is threatening the use of tactical nuclear weapons against Ukraine in case war's progress goes against Russia. It dangles this threat largely as a part of coercive diplomacy on its part. And yet, the realization of such a threat cannot be ruled out and is rightly regarded as a new and highly dangerous landmark in the evolution of the nuclear reality.

Furthermore, while the logic of MAD is very compelling also among smaller nuclear powers, arguably as much as it is between the superpowers, for some of these countries it might be less than absolute in certain extreme scenarios. Thus, if the Islamist regime in a future nuclear Iran goes down in a bloody revolution, will zealots in it resist the temptation to deliver a farewell nuclear strike, for example, against Israel or perhaps even the United States, actively seeking to bring about a general apocalypse? Similarly, can we be sure that the North Korean regime will not be tempted to use nuclear weapons under a perceived existential threat, real or imagined? We cannot remain complacent with respect to any such potential scenario.

With the exception of the five recognized nuclear powers, the 191 countries that have joined the Nuclear Non-Proliferation Treaty (NPT) since it was opened for signature in 1968 have agreed not to develop nuclear weapons and have accepted an inspection regime carried out by the International Atomic Energy Agency (IAEA). In return, they are entitled to free access to nuclear technologies for civilian use. The nuclear club, which in the early 1960s United States President John F. Kennedy apprehensively predicted would increase to fifteen to twenty by 1975, has shown only a modest expansion. Presently, it includes the five authorized nuclear members of the NPT (the United States, Soviet Union/Russia, China, Britain, and France), to which non-members Israel (undeclared), India, Pakistan, and North Korea have been added. A few other countries, such as South Africa, Brazil, Iraq, and Libya, had a clandestine military nuclear program at some point, in violation of their NPT commitment. Iran is currently engaged in such a program. If it decides to acquire the weapon, its neighbors in the Middle East, such as Saudi Arabia, Turkey, and Egypt, might follow suit.

Some scholars have argued that the spread of nuclear weapons should not be opposed and that it actually constitutes a good thing, as it would expand the same deterrence that prevailed between the superpowers during the Cold War to other regions of the world. However, critics of this view doubt that the logic of MAD is foolproof as nuclear weapons spread into a growing number of hands in less and less stable parts of the world. Such proliferation can indeed result in fewer wars owing to nuclear deterrence, but, by the same token, also in the eventual use of nuclear weapons—somewhere. Furthermore, since undeveloped countries possess far inferior technological and institutional infrastructures, the likelihood of an accidental use of nuclear weapons or of a nuclear accident is much greater.[22]

What both sides in this debate initially overlooked was the alarming prospect of nuclear terrorism, which we mentioned in the previous section. The few advocates of proliferation have later argued that states are very unlikely to compromise their control and hand over nuclear weapons to terrorists. However, as we have seen, the more significant risk in countries in which state institutions are weak, corruption is widespread, and organized crime is strong might be nuclear leakage. A threat from nuclear minnows such as terrorist organizations, unconstrained by mutual deterrence, may be evolving into a major concern.[23]

In conclusion, the ultimate weapon has nearly nullified the prospect of a major nuclear war between nuclear countries among which super-deterrence prevails. The uncertainty regarding possible gain from a war—the necessary precondition of war, touching on its very nature—is eliminated, as practically unhindered destructive power has been pushed to the very extreme. That said, even when the logic of MAD holds between nuclear states, their resulting restraint amounts to a 'negative peace'. It rests on the balance of terror, is conducive to arms races, and leaves room for covert, indirect, and low-intensity forms of armed conflict, perhaps even to direct limited war.

However, might war disappear and be replaced by a 'positive peace'—a disappearance of the very fear of war? Is war already declining? Or should these two propositions be dismissed as persistent delusions that contradict both human nature and the nature of war itself?

3

WAR

NOW AND FOREVER?

*The Nature of War and Human Nature:
Is War Inevitable?*

Are war and its nature, addressed in this book, intrinsic and irreducible parts of human nature? Is the very existence of war implied in its nature? While such a view has been rejected in philosophy with respect to God, our subject is more mundane.

The first thing to clarify concerns the past: has deadly human fighting, including highly lethal group warfare, always been with us? Or did it emerge later in our historical evolution, perhaps only with the adoption of agriculture or the rise of states? Were prehistoric humans living in nature warlike or peaceful? The two opposite views on this question are associated with the names of two famous thinkers: Thomas Hobbes, in the seventeenth century, claiming a violent aboriginal past, and Jean-Jacques Rousseau, a hundred years later, suggesting a peaceful one.[1] We shall not trace this centuries-long controversy here. Suffice it to say that the evidence that has come to light in recent decades leaves little doubt that humans have always fought viciously. Around 25 percent of all men in hunter-gatherer societies, before agriculture and the state, and perhaps 15 percent of the population, died violently, with the rest of the men covered in scars. Hobbes turns out to have been essentially right.[2]

Whether violence and war are in our nature is a question that bears on the future no less than on the past. Little wonder then that the biological underpinning of war and peace has been the subject of a heated debate and much confusion. The root of the confusion is this: people assume that if widespread deadly violence has always been with us, it must be a primary, 'irresistible' biological drive that is nearly impossible to suppress. They tend to believe that war is part of human nature and thus erupts in an almost irresistible way. This view is mistaken. Contrary to fashionable 1960s notions, traced back to Freud's latter-day theorizing about a death drive or instinct—*thanatos*—violence is not a primary drive that requires release like hunger or sex.[3] The Swiss or Swedes, for example, who have not fought for two centuries, show no special signs of deprivation on this account. But try to deny them food for more than a few hours, or sex, say, for more than a few days, and their reaction will be predictable enough.

Indeed, we do not need the cliché about the Swiss and the Swedes. The same thought experiment applies to the vast majority of people in the West, who live their entire life in peace and yet show no symptoms of deprivation of violence. Furthermore, that violence is not an elementary drive, a kind of compulsive impulse, is clearly demonstrated by the fact that people in different societies, or parts of society, exhibit extremely diverging levels of violence and violent death. Their appetites for food and sex, if not perhaps their ability to satisfy these appetites, are nowhere near as divergent amongst different societies.

On the other hand, the fact that violence is not a primary drive does not mean that we are not hardwired for it. Anthropologist Margaret Mead's framing of the problem, 'Warfare Is Only an Invention—Not a Biological Necessity' (1940), is the mother of all mistakes.[4] It expresses the widespread assumption that violence must be either a primary drive or entirely learned, whereas, in reality, its potential is deeply ingrained in us as a *means* or *tool*, ever-ready to be employed.

People can *cooperate, compete peacefully, or use violence* to achieve their objectives, depending on what they believe will serve them best in any given circumstance. In cooperation, the parties combine efforts, in principle because the synergic outcome of their efforts divided amongst them promises greater benefit to each of them than their independent efforts might. In competition, each party strives to outdo the other in order to achieve a desired good by employing whatever means they have at their disposal except direct action against the other. Competition runs parallel. By contrast, in a conflict, direct action against the competitor is taken in order to eliminate it or lessen its ability to engage in the competition.[5] Cooperation, competition, and conflict are the three fundamental forms of social interaction (in addition to avoidance or zero interaction). People have always had all three options to choose from, and they have always assessed the situation—intuitively or more deliberately—to decide which option, or combination of them, seemed the most promising. As individuals and as collectives, their choice is context-dependent, subject to what works in the particular social and historical conditions in which they live.

Thus, neither a late invention nor a compulsive inevitability independent of conditions, fighting—individually or in groups—is part of our evolution-shaped behavioral menu. People are well-equipped biologically for pursuing any of the above behavioral strategies, with conflict being only one tool, albeit a major one—the hammer—in our diverse behavioral toolkit. It is in this sense that *both* war and peace are 'in our genes', which accounts for their widely fluctuating prevalence in different socio-historical contexts. As the Seville Statement on Violence, issued in 1986 under the auspices of UNESCO, rightly puts it, in rejection of the view that human biology makes violence and war inescapable: 'There is nothing in our neurophysiology that compels us to react violently.... We conclude that biology does not condemn humanity to war.' However, the Statement fell into the opposite fallacy, proclaiming that warfare 'is a product of culture', and solemnly prescribing that *'IT IS SCIENTIFICALLY INCORRECT* to say that war or any other violent behavior is genetically programmed into our human nature' [emphasis in the original]. The Statement carelessly concluded, 'Violence is neither in our evolutionary legacy nor in our genes.'[6]

In reality, the potential for *both* war and peace is embedded in us. Although activated interchangeably and conjointly in response to the overall environmental and socio-cultural conditions, all three behavioral strategies—cooperation, peaceful competition, and violent conflict—are not *purely* learned cultural forms. The naive nature-nurture dichotomy overlooks the heavy and complex biological machinery that is necessary for the working of each of these behavioral strategies and the interplay between them. Certainly, these deep evolution-shaped patterns are variably calibrated to the particular conditions of the societies in which people live. However, the reason why they are all there, very close under our skin and readily activated, is that they were all very handy during our long evolutionary history. They all proved highly useful and advantageous, thereby becoming part and parcel of our biological equipment.

Wars have been fought for the attainment of the same objects of human desire that underlie the human motivational system in general—*only by violent means*, through the use of force. Here I take issue with Steven Pinker's excellent *The Better Angels of Our Nature* (2011), with which I am otherwise in much agreement. 'Angels' versus 'demons' in the human behavioral system is an allusion to Lincoln's first inaugural address and is largely invoked metaphorically. Yet not entirely, because Pinker points to particular human quests such as dominance or ideology as 'demons' with which the blame for war rests. However, dominance or ideology, no less than the desire for sex, can just as well be counted on the side of the 'angels' when pursued by peaceful means and for peaceful ends. For example, there have always been peaceful ideologies—such as Buddhism and, in principle, though all too often not in practice, Christianity—which preached peace as one of their central tenets.

The cause of war is not these or other human desires. Rather, violence and war occur when the conflictual behavioral strategy is judged to be more promising than peaceful competition and cooperation for achieving scarce objects of human desire. War is indeed a continuation of politics—the famous formula is of course true in the sense described earlier in the book; but politics itself is about the attainment and distribution of objects of human desire of all sorts, material and non-material. Thus, *both* our basic desires *and* the conditions that channel the efforts to fulfill them to the conflictual path are necessary for understanding why war occurs.

In this way, the advent of coercive state authority and state policing has tilted the menu of human behavioral strategies in the direction of the peaceful options in the domestic arena, bringing a great reduction in the rate of killings—in the form of homicide and blood revenge—within societies. Thomas Hobbes was generally right about this. Moreover, changing economic, social, and political conditions have been generating a similar effect in the international arena, most notably where a modern liberal economic and political order prevails and peaceful behavioral options become much more rewarding than the violent option in achieving unprecedented levels of affluence and comfort.

Is War Declining—Why and Where?

The Russian invasion of Ukraine in 2022 and the ensuing large-scale war brought back with a vengeance the question of whether the world was becoming more peaceful.[7] This proposition had in any case been met with widespread disbelief. After all, in the decades preceding the war in Ukraine, the United States and its allies were repeatedly involved in messy local wars. Furthermore, the relative peacefulness of the post-Cold War decades has been widely attributable to a transient American hegemony. Have we not been tempted by a resurfacing of old illusions of peace that are dispelled by a resurgent Russia, by the rise of China to superpower status, and by vicious wars in South and Central Asia, the Middle East, and Africa? With the war in Ukraine and the growing threats of war around Taiwan and in the South China Sea, so-called 'realists' in international relations theory have been able to raise their heads again and claim that they had told you so.[8] Yet they have missed the main point and compare apples with cabbage. There has been understandable shock about war occurring in the 'middle of Europe'. But the real dividing lines are not a matter of a particular continent or 'race'.

Today's world is divided into two very distinct zones: a 'zone of peace' encompassing all the developed countries, those with nominal GDP per capita higher than $20,000 from non-oil and gas sources (not indicative of development); and a 'zone of war', which includes developing or undeveloped countries, as well as failed developers, whose GDP per capita is lower, often much lower, than this threshold.[9]

The 'zone of war', where war and the threat of war are very much alive, is all too familiar. It extends from the borders of China (some $12,000 GDP per capita) and North Korea, through South and Central Asia and the Indian subcontinent, to the Caucasus, to Russia's borders (GDP per capita fluctuating with the price of energy, and in any case relatively low and derived from material resources), to the

Middle East and North Africa (a few thousand dollars per capita in the non-oil producing countries), to sub-Saharan Africa (in many cases no more than a few hundred dollars per capita). In all these areas, war is rife or looming, mostly civil wars, but also inter-state wars.

By contrast, awareness of the 'zone of peace' is distracted by the persistent involvement of the United States and its allies in wars in the less developed parts of the world. Such involvement has been prompted by direct threats arising from these parts (the War on Terror, Afghanistan), but also includes interventions in local conflicts that disrupt the liberal world order (Iraq), as well as humanitarian interventions (Somalia, Kosovo, and Libya). After all, it can scarcely be argued that the United States waged these wars for profit. On the contrary, it has lost a great deal in treasure, life, and prestige.

More significantly, whereas the undeveloped or developing areas are a clear war zone—within themselves and irrespective of foreign involvement—the developed world is an absolute zone of peace. While the United States' recent wars in the world's 'zone of war' attract all the attention, it is scarcely asked why Canada is not at all concerned about the prospect of being conquered by the United States, which would have increased American wealth and power considerably, even more, one assumes, than a war in Afghanistan. People find it difficult to explain why exactly this is so. Similarly, Holland and Belgium no longer fear a German (or French) invasion in the slightest, a historically unprecedented situation. In East Asia, outside the West, the most developed countries, such as Japan, South Korea, and Taiwan—even though, for historical reasons relating to Japan's colonial past, there is no love lost between them—do not fear war among themselves, or with any of the other developed countries. At the same time, they are deeply apprehensive of being attacked by less developed neighbors, such as China or North Korea. That Australia and New Zealand do not fear each other seems so obvious that it attracts no special attention. Latin America has been noted as a borderline case—not quite developed and yet relatively peaceful, especially as concerns inter-state wars, if not civil wars.[10]

Thus, the probability of war amongst developed, affluent liberal democracies has declined to a vanishing point, where they no longer even see the need to prepare for the *possibility* of a militarized dispute with one another. The 'security dilemma'—better termed 'insecurity', the fear of the other by virtue of its very existence and potentially aggressive intent—which is an ostensibly intrinsic feature of international anarchy according to 'realists', no longer exists among them. Much the same applies to civil wars. Modernized, economically developed democracies in today's world have become practically free of civil wars—on account of their stronger consensual nature, plurality, tolerance, and, moreover, a greater legitimacy for peaceful

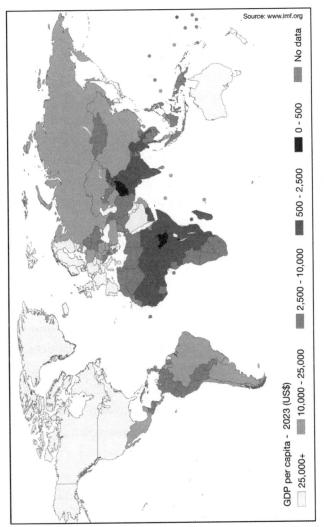

Figure 1: Zones of Peace, Zones of War

secession. Thus, all forms of war, and the fear of war itself, have disappeared within the developed parts of the world. In contrast to the 'negative' peace of mutual nuclear deterrence, these parts enjoy an unprecedented 'positive' peace, in which war is not even perceived as an option.

What explains these most salient realities? While the glaring peace phenomenon is far from being universally recognized, several explanations have been around to account for various aspects of it. We shall examine the validity and limitations of each of them and seek to elucidate the more comprehensive rationale underlying the 'zone of peace'.

The so-called Long Peace among the great powers—no war between the great powers since 1945—is widely recognized and commonly attributed to the nuclear balance of terror, a decisive factor to be sure that concentrated the minds of all involved wonderfully, as they say about the hanging rope.[11] The absence of war between democracies has been equally recognized. However, the decrease in war had been well-marked even before the nuclear era and had encompassed both democracies and non-democracies. Between 1815 and 1914, wars between the great powers, as well as between other industrializing countries, declined in frequency to about a *third* of what they had been in previous centuries—an unprecedented change. Austria and Prussia, for example, neither of them a democracy, fought about a

WAR, NOW AND FOREVER?

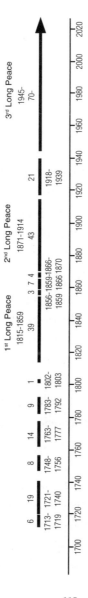

Figure 2: The 'Long Peace' Phenomenon since 1815

third to a quarter as many wars after 1815 as they had in the preceding century.[12]

The Long Peace between the great powers since 1945 has endured for seventy-nine years at the time of writing and counting (with the partial exception of the United States–China clash in Korea 1950–1953, China's entry into the great power league). However, it was preceded by the second longest peace ever, without wars occurring amongst the great powers between 1871 and 1914, forty-three years in all (again, with the possible exception of the Russo-Japanese War 1904–1905, Japan's ticket into the great power league); and by the third longest peace between 1815 and 1854, totaling thirty-nine years. The nineteenth century has long been recognized as by far the most peaceful in European history until then. Thus, the three longest periods of peace in the modern great power system have all occurred since 1815, with each of these periods longer than the preceding one, and with the first two taking place *before* the nuclear age. Rather than with the familiar Long Peace, we are dealing with a Long Peace *phenomenon*. Notably, no similar long periods of peace occurred in the modern great power system before 1815.

In response, it is sometimes claimed that colonial wars during the nineteenth century and 'wars by proxy' in the twentieth century have substituted for great power wars. While space is too limited to respond to this claim, the fact remains that great power wars themselves, the most massive and destructive in history, have sharply decreased in their occurrence, an unprecedented change. In explaining this, we need to address the entire unique period of reduced belligerency from 1815 onward, long before the bomb. At the same time, it is necessary to account for the glaring and colossal exception to the trend: the two world wars.

If the nuclear factor cannot explain the first and second long periods of peace amongst the great powers during the nineteenth century, maybe it is the lethality, destructiveness, and economic cost of modern *conventional* wars that account for the trend. This hypothesis barely holds, however, because relative to population and wealth, wars have not become more lethal and costly than they were in earlier times. The wars from 1815 to 1914 were, in fact, particularly light. Prussia won the wars of German unification in short and decisive campaigns and at a remarkably low price, and yet Germany did not fight again for forty-three years. The world wars, especially World War II, were certainly on the upper end of the scale in terms of casualties; yet, contrary to widespread assumptions, they were far from being exceptional in history. We need to look at *relative* casualties—the percentage of those dying in wars in each society—rather than at the aggregate created by the fact that many states participated in the world wars.

In the Peloponnesian War (431–403 BCE), for example, Athens is estimated to have lost between a quarter and a third of its population, more than Germany in the two world wars *combined*.[13] In the first three years of the Second Punic War (218–216 BCE), Rome lost some 50,000 male citizens of military age, out of a total of about 200,000.[14] This was roughly 25 percent in only three years, the same range as the Soviet military casualties and higher than the German rates in World War II. Similarly, in the thirteenth century, the Mongol conquests inflicted casualties and destruction on the societies of China and Russia that were among the highest ever suffered during historical times. Even by the lowest estimates casualties were at least as high as, and in China almost definitely far higher than, the Soviet Union's horrific rate in World War II of about 15 percent of its population.[15] A final example: during the Thirty Years War (1618–1648) population loss in Germany is estimated at between a fifth and a third—either way again higher than the German casualties in the First and Second World Wars *combined*.[16]

The strong intuition we have that more developed military technology during modern times must mean greater lethality and destructiveness is misleading, for modern technology also means greater *protective* power, as with mechanized armor, mechanized speed and agility, and electronic defensive measures. Offensive and defensive technologies generally rise in tandem and tend to offset each other. In addition, it is all too often forgotten that the vast majority of the many millions of non-combatants killed by Germany during World War II—Jews, Soviet prisoners of war, Soviet civilians—fell victim to intentional starvation, exposure to the elements, and mass executions rather than to any sophisticated military technology. Instances of genocide in general during the twentieth century, much as earlier in history, were carried out with the simplest of technologies, as the Rwandan genocide horrifically reminded us.

Nor is it true that wars during the past two centuries have become economically more costly than they were earlier in history, again relative to overall wealth. War always involved massive economic exertion and was the single most expensive item of state spending.[17] Both sixteenth- and seventeenth century Spain and eighteenth-century France, for example, were economically ruined by war and staggering war debts, which in the French case brought about the Revolution. Furthermore, death by starvation in premodern wars was widespread. Consider Yemen and parts of Africa today.

If wars have not become more lethal, destructive, and costly, what then is the cause of the decline in belligerency? Even before the middle of the nineteenth century, during the first Long Peace, thinkers such as Saint-Simon, Auguste Comte, and John Stuart Mill realized that it was caused by the advent of the Industrial Revolution, the most profound transformation of human society since the transition to agriculture from some 10,000 years ago onward.[18] Above all, the Industrial Revolution led to explosive growth in per

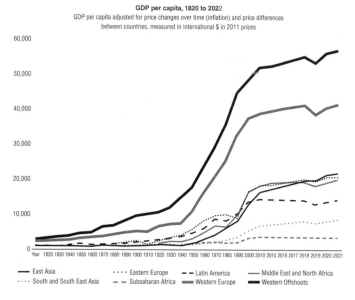

Figure 3

capita wealth, about thirty- to fifty-fold from the onset of the revolution to the present in the countries that have gone through the revolution. Thus, the trap that had plagued premodern societies, famously described by British demographer Thomas Malthus's *Essay on the Principle of Population* (1798), whereby slow growth in wealth was absorbed by more children and more mouths to feed, has been broken. Wealth no longer constitutes a fundamentally finite quantity and a zero-sum game, when the only question is how it is divided, and with force functioning as a major means of attaining a larger share of a fixed pie. Since the outbreak of the Industrial Revolution, the pie has been continuously growing, and wealth has now been derived predominantly from economic growth and investment at home, from which war tends to be a wasteful distraction. The entire rationale of wealth creation and acquisition has been transformed.

Scholars have rightly pointed to the much-increased significance of trade and economic interdependence as the cause of peace.[19] However, trade has ballooned to entirely new dimensions, and greater freedom of trade has become all the more attractive, precisely *because* of the process of industrialization. The reason for this is that the overwhelming share of fast-growing and diversifying production in the industrial age has been intended for sale in the marketplace rather than for direct consumption by the peasant producers themselves, as in preindustrial times. Consequently, economies are no longer overwhelmingly local and autarkic, having become increasingly interconnected by specialization, scale, and exchange on a national and international scale. Foreign devastation potentially depresses the entire system and is detrimental to a state's own well-being. What John Stuart Mill discerned in the abstract in the 1840s was repeated by Norman Angell during the first global age before World War I, and it formed the cornerstone of John Maynard Keynes's criticism of the harsh reparations imposed on Germany after World War I.[20]

Keynes argued that if the German economy was not allowed to revive, the global economy could not recover either. This was a matter of self-interest for the victors.

Greater economic openness has also decreased the likelihood of war by disassociating economic access from the confines of political borders and sovereignty. It is no longer necessary to politically possess a territory in order to benefit from it. Of all these factors, commercial interdependence has attracted the most attention in the scholarly literature. But it is the escape from the Malthusian Trap with rapid industrial growth that has been the underlying cause of both commercial interdependence and free trade, of what is best described as the Modernization Peace.

Thus, the greater the yield of competitive economic cooperation, the more counterproductive and less attractive conflict becomes. *Rather than war becoming more costly, as is widely believed, it is in fact peace that has been growing more profitable.*

The claim that democracies do not fight each other is another much-cited explanation for the peace, massively supported by the evidence from the nineteenth century to the present. Moreover, in today's world, all the economically developed countries are democratic. However, if so, how can we distinguish between the effects of economic development and those of democratization in reducing belligerency? In considering this question, the following needs to be borne in mind: first, premodern democracies, as in ancient Greece and Italy, fought each other viciously; it is only when the entire rationale of wealth acquisition changed with modernization that modern democracies ceased to do so. Second, as already noted, non-democracies have also fought much less during the industrial age, compared to earlier times. Third, the spread of democracy itself has been a result of the process of modernization, with the urbanization, growing literacy, expanding middle class, and extensive communications that it brought in its wake. Note that no democracy on a large country-level scale, beyond the city-state or canton size, had existed *ever* and *anywhere* before modernity. Similarly, it is no coincidence that the overwhelming majority of democracies in today's world are developed countries. Thus, both economic interdependence and democracy—cited as the causes for the increasing peacefulness—are actually a function of, and ride on, the process of industrial-technological modernization.

That said, although non-liberal and non-democratic states also became much less belligerent during the industrial age, it is the liberal democracies that have been the most attuned to its pacifying aspects. Relying on arbitrary coercive force at home, nondemocratic countries have found it more natural to use force abroad. By contrast, liberal democratic societies are socialized to peaceful, law-mediated relations at home, and their citizens have grown to expect that the same norms be applied internationally. Living in increasingly tolerant societies, they have grown more receptive to the Other's point of view. Promoting freedom, legal equality, and political participation domestically, liberal democratic powers—although initially in possession of vast empires—have found it increasingly difficult to justify ruling over foreign peoples without their consent. And sanctifying life, liberty, and human rights, they have proven to be failures in forceful repression. Furthermore, with the individual's life and pursuit of happiness elevated above group values, sacrifice of life in war has increasingly lost legitimacy in liberal democratic societies. War retains legitimacy only under steadily narrowing conditions and is generally viewed as extremely abhorrent and undesirable.

If the entire rationale of war and peace has been transformed and tilted towards the peaceful options, why have wars continued to occur during the past two centuries, albeit at a much lower frequency? First, ethnic and nationalist tensions—people's desire to live with their kin-culture community in an independent state—have often overridden the logic of the new economic realities, accounting for most wars in Europe between 1815 and 1945.[21] Consider the wars that separated the first and second Long Peace. With the exception of the Crimean War (1854–1856), these were the War of 1859 that led to Italy's unification, and the Wars of German Unification (1864, 1866, 1870–1871). Ethnic and nationalist tensions continue to be the main cause of war today, especially in the less developed parts of the globe.

Moreover, nationalism was a major contributing factor in the retreat from free trade into national economies during the late nineteenth and early twentieth centuries, as the new industrial great powers—the United States, Germany, Japan, and France—resumed protectionism. They raised tariffs to shelter their nascent industries from British industrial dominance. This led to the return of imperialism from 1882 on.

People at the time realized that 'imperialism does not pay'. Africa, the main scene of the imperialist race, constituted only 1–2 percent of world trade; the main objection to imperial expansion came from the British Treasury, where it was clear that colonies involved only costs and little profit; Britain and France, the leading imperial powers, were also those that contracted the most in their share of the world economy between 1870 and 1914. Still, growing protectionism meant that the emergent global economy might become partitioned rather than open, with each imperial domain becoming closed to everybody else. Although colonial territories in Africa had close to no economic value, they might become valuable decades or centuries later, after development, when it would be too late to acquire them. A snowball effect ensued, as each power hastened to grab what it could, while it could.[22]

The size of a nation makes little difference in an open international economy. The citizens of little Luxembourg are as rich as, or richer than, the citizens of the United States. By contrast, size becomes the key to economic success in a closed, neo-mercantilist international economy, because small countries cannot possibly produce everything by themselves. Moreover, in a partitioned global economy, economic power increases national strength, while national strength defends and increases economic power. It again becomes necessary to politically own a territory in order to profit from it.

Therefore, tensions heightened between the great powers associated with the imperialist race, eventually leading to World War I. That change was completed in the 1930s, with the Great Depression, as the United States, Britain, and France practically closed their territories and empires to imports by high tariffs. For the territorially confined Germany and Japan, the need to break out into an imperial *Lebensraum* or 'East Asian Co-Prosperity Sphere' seemed particularly pressing. Here lay the seeds of the two world wars. Furthermore, the retreat from economic liberalism spurred, and was spurred on by, the rise to power of anti-liberal and anti-democratic political ideologies and regimes that incorporated a creed of violence: communism and fascism.

Since 1945, the decline of major war has deepened further. Nuclear weapons, the institutionalization of free trade, and the closely related process of rapid and sustained economic growth, as well as the spread of liberal democracy, have all contributed to this trend. The liberal economic and political world order gained further momentum after the collapse of the Soviet Union and the end of the Cold War. Indeed, American hegemony has been widely cited as the explanation for the ensuing decades of peace. 'Realists' have even claimed that this applies to Western Europe and explain why their post-Cold War prophecies of 'Back to the Future' concerning the return of armed rivalry to Western Europe, German acquisition of nuclear weapons, and so on, have failed to materialize.[23] However, while American hegemony has been a cardinal factor, it is far from being the root cause of the peace. Consider that the United States, in its role as the 'world's policeman' has failed to enforce peace in large parts of the developing and undeveloped world. The notion that a present-day Germany of eighty million people is constrained by American hegemony from reasserting itself as an armed militant power should be recognized as the preposterous idea that it is. The United States could scarcely enforce much even in Iraq or Afghanistan. Countries in all parts of the developed world, including Western Europe, are simply as interested in peaceful development as the United States is. Without exception, they are as much a part of the 'positive' peace of mutual economic growth and prosperity, involving the unprecedented disappearance of the fear of war itself within all the developed parts of the world. Indeed, the societies of Western Europe are actually *more* pacifist than the United States.

This brings us to the darker and more dangerous parts of the picture. The dramatic spread of peace, while very real, is far from being foolproof and free from shadows and challenges. As noted, one threat that is likely to hang over our heads during the twenty-first century is the prospect of unconventional terrorism. An even greater threat is the return of a regime type—authoritarian–capitalist—that had been absent from the international system since the defeat of Germany and Japan in 1945.

Transformed from a backward communist economy to a fast-developing authoritarian–capitalist great power—communist in name only—China is now recognized to represent the greatest challenge to the liberal world order. Russia, too, has been retreating from its post-communist liberalism and has assumed an increasingly authoritarian and nationalist character, coupled with a more aggressive stance. During the high tide of democratic optimism, I suggested that although the new authoritarian–capitalist great powers, most notably China, were deeply integrated into the world economy, there existed the prospect of more antagonistic relations with the democratic world, accentuated ideological rivalry, potential and actual conflict, intensified arms races, and new cold wars. Critics argued in response that China was bound to join the liberal world order, as well as liberalize itself.[24] Needless to say, since then China and Russia have become more authoritarian and oppressive domestically—present-day China and Russia may even be labeled semi-totalitarian. Simultaneously, they have become far more assertive and aggressive internationally.

Moreover, since the outbreak of the economic crisis in 2007–2008 and the subsequent upheavals in the democracies, the authoritarian great powers have gained much confidence, while the hegemony and prestige of democratic capitalism have suffered a massive blow unparalleled since the 1930s and the rise of fascist and communist totalitarianism. One hopes that the current economic and political malaise in the democracies will not be nearly as catastrophic.

Will China become more assertive and aggressive as its wealth and power increase during the coming decades? Or, on the contrary, will its growing affluence, crossing the threshold for a developed country (in today's values, rising from $12,000 to about $20,000 GDP per capita) make China's people, and government, more liberal and increasingly averse to military action, as is the case throughout the developed world? Given China's size, might, and historical traditions, this is, in my opinion, an open question—indeed, the premier political question of the twenty-first century.

The prospect of renewed protectionism, fueled by new military tensions, increases the likelihood of armed confrontation, as production and trade are again linked to territory and direct rule. The system of free trade has been exploited by China, such as in the direct theft of knowledge, the coercion of foreign companies to cede know-how, and a policy of hidden subsidies to its exports. But the main threat is the use of wealth derived from the system of peaceful free trade to exert political-military pressure, including the threat and use of war. As Adam Smith, the theorist and champion of free trade, has put it: 'Defence is much more important than opulence'.[25] On the other hand, if protectionism and trade blocs are going to re-emerge, China's incentive to secure its control over vital resources, as in the South China Sea and Taiwan, might grow momentously. There is no easy solution to this bind.

Russia is a country lacking a truly productive sector, whose international trade is limited mostly to the export of energy and other raw materials, and whose power of attraction towards its neighbors/former imperial domains is low. It is left only with the threat and use of arms as its main foreign policy tool vis-à-vis its neighbors, who are trying to escape its embrace. This is how it was with Georgia, and later with Ukraine.

To sum up, war has been declining and, indeed, has entirely disappeared in all its forms within the developed world. This is an unprecedented and hugely optimistic development. But the deeper causes of peace in the modernization development sphere and, hence, the boundaries of the 'zone of peace' must be clearly understood so as to calibrate our expectations and prepare us for the rough times ahead. The war in Ukraine—like the wars in Africa, the Middle East, and potentially the Indian subcontinent and around China and North Korea—demonstrate that the world's less developed 'zone of war' is still simmering and occasionally erupts into destructive and lethal armed conflicts. Indeed they might even involve the use of nuclear weapons—in Ukraine, if Russia loses, and elsewhere.

In conclusion, neither human nature nor the nature of war itself make war—the wide-scale use of collective lethal violence—a necessity, as many assume. The potential for violence to achieve our ends is indeed biologically embedded in us, as one of the tools in our behavioral toolkit, side by side with peaceful cooperation and non-violent competition. Which of these tools is resorted to depends on our assessment of the conditions at hand—social, cultural, and historical. This explains why levels of lethal violence are not equal or constant, but rather diverge widely between societies and segments of societies. It also helps to explain why war in all its forms, and the fear of war itself, have wholly disappeared within the developed parts of the world, where the entire rationale of benefit acquisition has sharply veered towards the peaceful options.

CONCLUSION

The quest for a theory of war—and with it the question of what exactly it is, and the strong expectation that it be universal—has gained new, much-enhanced significance since the eighteenth-century Enlightenment. There are two main reasons for this: it was during that time, following the scientific revolution a century earlier, crowned by Newtonian physics, that the quest for a general theory in every field of reality and every discipline grew supreme. At the same time, the view that theory should be universal in form achieved dominance precisely because the people of that period had become acutely aware of historical transformation—a new realization—and expected theory to encompass and transcend change.

The notion of the 'classic' has gone hand in hand with this expectation and has a strong hold on our mind. The 'classic' is mostly understood as a work that touches on deep truths about the world and us. For this reason, it remains relevant and present, stimulating the intellectual discourse over the ages, despite the often far-reaching changes of time and circumstances. 'Classics' are a repository of ideas and scraps of ideas that can find their place in the construction of subsequent intellectual edifices. Plato and Aristotle are iconic examples of this. Alternatively, a 'classic' is perceived as a work that most strikingly and prominently represented a certain age and worldview, and hence played a major role in the consciousness of that and later ages, even if the worldview in question is no longer deemed that relevant today. Possible examples are the works of St. Augustine or Thomas Aquinas for non-religious or even non-Catholic people at present.

So what are the classic works of military theory, and what makes them classical? Clausewitz's work has gained the status of a universal theory, to no small degree because of a failure to understand what exactly he meant, which, as mentioned earlier, has given rise to an Emperor's New Clothes syndrome. Sun Tzu's *The Art of War*, with its traditional aphoristic and metaphorical Chinese style, has also won such a status—including, somewhat amusingly, in current business guidebooks. More than others, his slim volume, although rooted in the realities of military organization in Warring States China some 2,500 years ago, has captured what are felt to be fundamental truths about war and its conduct. Translated and discovered in the West in the twentieth century, it has been accepted with well-deserved admiration. In addition, quite a few military authors were significant and relevant in their own and later times, though much less so eventually, as the historical militaries and conduct of war they described have become a thing of the past. Examples include Xenophon, Caesar, Vegetius, Machiavelli, Guibert, and Jomini. Closer to the present, the writings of Mahan and Corbett, Fuller and Liddell Hart, and arguably Douhet, are also widely regarded as classical texts in one form or another. But, indeed, are they classics in the first, universalist sense, or in the second, more time-bound meaning?

Before returning to this question, we note that the notion of the 'classic' is often perceived somewhat naively. Does psychology, for example, dealing with human nature itself, have its classics in the universalist sense? The layperson may name Freud, but despite his huge cultural impact during the twentieth century, his ideas have been largely discredited and are cited today mainly as intellectual history or in so-called cultural studies. Economics—like war, a field of practical application on a grand scale—has a better claim for a living classic: Adam Smith and his *Wealth of Nations* (1776). To a lesser degree perhaps, the same category may also include David Ricardo, John Maynard Keynes, Friedrich Hayek, and Milton Friedman. However, one does not have to be a Marxist to hold, for example as Karl Polanyi does, that economies, and with them economic theories, are 'socially embedded'; that they have transformed momentously with changing historical conditions. Thus, rather than timeless, the above-mentioned modern classics of economic theory have formulated in the language of theory the major historical transformation of modernity: first, the nascent capitalist economy emerging in early modern Britain, and, later, the constitutive features of the new industrial and global economy. This has been a tremendous theoretical achievement that has served us well (though obviously not perfectly) in navigating modern economic realities.

Economic theory regularly takes an abstract form and expresses itself in the language of general principles. There is no harm in this, as human cognition works by coining abstract concepts to capture a fluctuating reality. Indeed, abstract modelling has gained the upper hand in economic theory over the last decades. Quantitative values, such as money and other measurable variables, particularly present in, and characteristic of, the field of economics, reinforce this trend. Still, the debate within economics between more abstract-oriented and history-oriented approaches continues.[1] Some major concepts of economic theory can surely be regarded as fundamental to the field, including scarcity as the underlying rationale of the discipline, the relationship between demand and supply, the role of self-interest, and the regulating mechanism of benefit-seeking. But the bulk of economic doctrine—both its theory and practical principles—consists of a myriad of time-bound minutiae: large and small pieces of knowledge, insights, and rules of thumb, all generalized from practical experience—of long-, medium-, or short-term historical validity and applicability.

Obviously, there are differences between various fields of human activity and knowledge, such as economics and strategy, for example as to how quantitative they are. Still, where does the above leave us with respect to the feasibility of a universal theory of war and its conduct—valid across time and applying to diverse conditions and changing historical circumstances? We have argued in this book that the scope of such a theory is very limited. As Clausewitz suggested—even if he seriously erred in some of his major inferences in this regard—the constitutive features of war and human fighting are, so to speak, analytically implicit in war's 'nature'. Such analytical distinctions, 'by definition', are regarded in philosophy as formal and empty in the sense that they add no new content or information to what is already implicit in the original concept. However, as we have seen, they may shed light on major features of the phenomenon in question that are not always clear or self-evident, as well as have some very practical implications in the conduct of war.

Let us recapitulate. The two-way interrelationship between 'political' ends and 'military' means in war is logically derived from what the concepts of ends and means signify. Practically, this implies that the desired 'political' ends and the 'military' means employed to attain them must be harmonized, which may require adaptations on *both* sides of the means–ends equation. Similarly, the notion of victory and what it signifies can be analytically derived from the 'nature of war', and yet what victory means has been far from self-evident or well-recognized. The deep-seated view that victory means crushing the enemy's ability to resist so that a political settlement of whatever kind can be imposed on him has often led to active resistance by the military to political 'interference' in the conduct of war. As MacArthur put it, 'In war there is no substitute for victory'. However, after some bitter experiences, another, different understanding of what victory could mean has been increasingly recognized: the attainment of the war's political ends, with the understanding that these two notions of victory often do not quite overlap and sometimes conflict.

The relationship between defense and attack can similarly be analytically derived from the 'nature of war'. The distinction between these two forms of war is best characterized by their respective relation to the status quo: one aims to preserve while the other aims to change it. Clausewitz got this right, while getting everything else about the subject wrong. He failed to see that the power relations between defense and attack, rather than being anchored in the 'nature of war', depend on a variety of circumstances and factors—some of which, under certain conditions, can work in favor of the defense, and some in favor of the attack.

CONCLUSION

Other central features of war are rooted in strong propensities closely associated with the activity of fighting as an adversarial and deadly contest. They include, inter alia, the element of fear in the face of the danger of death, which calls for the qualities of courage, fighting spirit, or morale; the 'fog of war'; the non-linear logic of the conduct of military operations; the combined significance of brute force, cunning, deception-surprise, and similar means to throw the other side off balance; initiative and a resolute and vigorous/bold action, which should not become recklessness; and a balancing act between sticking to the objective and flexibility, and between concentration of force, economy of force, and security. Most of these features have been generalized in the so-called 'principles of war', a concept and term inherited from the Enlightenment. While their content has changed to the very abstract form it assumed in the twentieth century, the name, the 'principles of war', and their universalist claim—better supported by the current principles' general but necessarily less concrete content—have remained.

Still, most of what puts flesh on the bones of military theory is time-bound, relating to broad yet particular historical conditions: technological, economic, social, political, and cultural. Shifting conditions shape what are known as 'doctrines' of various time ranges—short, medium, or long. As we have seen, three or four major technological revolutions have taken place since the advent of the industrial age, transforming human reality, including war. Successively, they centered on the steam and iron revolution of the nineteenth century; the internal combustion engine, electric engine, and chemicals of the Second Industrial Revolution from the late nineteenth century onward; and the electronic-computers revolution after 1945, eventually opening up the entire field of cyberwarfare and AI. To this should be added the even more far-reaching revolution of nuclear weapons. There have thus been, for example, doctrines of trench warfare, armored warfare, air warfare, and electronic-computerized warfare. There have been distinct doctrines of naval warfare for the oar, sail, and steam ages, as well as for the dreadnought, aircraft carrier, and missile eras. All such categories and many sub-categories were in their times stable and enduring enough to serve as crucial guidance for the activity of fighting. But they also evolved, transformed, and disappeared altogether, with new 'categories' emerging to form the main body of military doctrine, training, and the conduct of operations.

Devotees to the 'principles of war' hold that the various doctrines apply the universal to the specific conditions covered by each particular doctrine. While this view is fine as far as it goes, remember that the 'principles of war' contain major tensions and contradictions that we accept because we recognize the value of each of these often-contrasting precepts. We have mentioned tensions such as those existing between brute force and cunning, or direct and indirect strategy, and the qualities of the lion and the fox; between sticking to the objective, on the one hand, and, on the other, flexibility with respect to both the military goals and political aims of the war; and between concentration of force, economy of force, and security. Under this very broad umbrella, the principles ostensibly cover both Napoleon's crushing victories, and Wellington's scorched earth and defensive ones, as well as evasive guerrilla warfare, and what not. A vast diversity of military practices can fit into the concept of the 'principles of war'.

Thus, the abstract 'principles of war'—the 'dazzling flashes of the self-evident'—should be taken seriously, but not too seriously. They reflect the two faces of the way our mind works: we formulate concepts as cognitive frameworks that allow us to cope successfully with the infiniteness of reality; and then, in what is known as 'reification' or 'metaphysication', we tend to identify the concepts with reality, sometimes substituting them for reality, and regard them as set in stone rather than as adaptive and flexible generalized schemas of our mind. As already mentioned, there is nothing wrong with this or with the quest for and template of the 'universal', as long as one does not become too pedantic. Remember that theory does not stop things from happening. Indeed, as we have seen, the very existence of war itself is not necessarily fixed in the nature of reality, as many would have it. Indisputably, violence and human violence, including collective violence, are very strong propensities. However, their prevalence, intensity, and, indeed, forms vary radically under different conditions, reaching extremely lethal levels under some, while declining close to a vanishing point under others.

Frederick the Great was reportedly frustrated by his dashing cavalry commander Friedrich Wilhelm von Seydlitz's indifference to the seminars in military theory, which the learned king, a leading exponent of the Enlightenment, found necessary to impart on his senior commanders. Yet, when the Seven Years' War came, none of this prevented Seydlitz's cavalry from smashing the French army at Rossbach (1757) and playing a decisive role in all the other great battles of the war. Similarly, the once very mediocre student in the United States Military Academy at West Point, Ulysses S. Grant, told a young officer after becoming famous that he had never paid much attention to military theory (Jomini). 'The art of war', he said, 'is simple enough. Find out where your enemy is. Get at him as soon as you can. Strike him as hard as you can, and keep moving on.'[2] In this, one might say, Grant himself in effect articulated a theory for the conduct of military operations, which, one might add, actually rings all too familiar. He also reminded us how elementary the theory of war is, especially in its abstract parts, before it is fully dressed with the innumerable details, great and small, of practical experience, the ocean of

CONCLUSION

concrete conditions of armament and organization, and the specifics of military doctrines.

Inferences from the 'nature of war'—the analytical dissection of what is implied in the concept of wide-scale and lethal collective violence—often turn out to have crucial practical value in the planning and execution of war. Similarly, the 'principles of war' help in focusing military education and operational planning on some key, partly contrasting, insights generated from the experience of war and the wisdom of the ages. At the same time, it is our circumstantial reason, as expressed in the diversity of ever-changing doctrines, that assesses what the main threats of war at present are; what forms—shaped by political, social, economic, cultural, and technological conditions—it might take; and what the optimal means in terms of military organization, training, and fighting should be. These questions and dilemmas have always been, and still are, of the highest order.

NOTES

INTRODUCTION

1. See my *The Origins of Military Thought: From the Enlightenment to Clausewitz* (Oxford: Clarendon Press, 1989); incorporated into my *A History of Military Thought: From the Enlightenment to the Cold War* (Oxford: Oxford University Press, 2001).
2. Niccolò Machiavelli, *The Art of War*. In Allen Gilbert (ed.), *The Chief Works and Others* (Durham: Duke University Press, 1965), vol. i, pp. 597, 625, 632, 634, 637.
3. For a fuller treatment of Machiavelli, with references, see the 'Introduction' chapter to my volumes above (n. 1).
4. Although influential military thinker Jean Charles, Chevalier de Folard, came close to this in his *Histoire de Polybe* (1724–30).
5. Jean Colin, *L'Infanterie au XVIII e siècle* (Paris: Chapelot, 1907), and Robert Quimby, *The Background of Napoleonic Warfare* (New York: Columbia University Press, 1957), are still useful.
6. J. A. H. Guibert, *A General Essay on Tactics* (London: T. Egerton, 1781; French original, 1772), p. 1.
7. Ibid., pp. 2–3.
8. Ibid., p. 99.
9. See the chapter on Jomini (4.ii) in my books above (n. 1).
10. J. F. C. Fuller, 'The Principles of War, with Reference to the

Campaigns of 1914–1915', *Journal of the Royal United Service Institution* 61:3 (1916). For an exhaustive history of the principles (which is at the same time entirely unaware of the historical-intellectual background), see John Alger, *The Quest for Victory: The History of the Principles of War* (Westport: Greenwood Press, 1982).

11. Carl von Clausewitz, *Strategie aus dem Jahre 1804, mit Zusätzen von 1808 und 1809* (Hamburg: Hanseatische Verlagsanstalt, 1943), 1808, section 29, p. 46.
12. Ibid., 1809, section 33, pp. 60–61.
13. Carl von Clausewitz, *On War*, ed. and trans. Michael Howard and Peter Paret (Princeton: Princeton University Press, 1976), p. 70.
14. See the part on Clausewitz in my books cited in n. 1; followed, in an updated and expanded form, by my *The Clausewitz Myth: Or the Emperor's New Clothes* (London: Chronos Books, 2024).
15. Thomas Schelling, *The Strategy of Conflict* (Cambridge MA: Harvard University Press, 1960); *Arms and Influence* (New Haven, CT: Yale University Press, 1966).

1. THE NATURE OF WAR

1. 'Note of 10 July 1827', in *On War*, p. 69.
2. Martin van Creveld, *The Transformation of War* (New York: Free Press, 1991); John Keegan, *A History of Warfare* (New York: Alfred A. Knopf, 1993). Also, John Mueller, *The Remnants of War* (Ithaca: Cornell University Press, 2004); Mary Kaldor, *New and Old Wars: Organized Violence in a Global Era* (Cambridge: Polity Press, 2012).
3. Azar Gat, *War in Human Civilization* (Oxford: Oxford University Press, 2006); idem, 'Proving Communal Warfare among Hunter-Gatherers: The Quasi-Rousseauan Error', *Evolutionary Anthropology*, 24 (2015) pp. 111–126; idem, *The*

Causes of War and the Spread of Peace: But Will War Rebound? (Oxford: Oxford University Press, 2017).

4. Azar Gat, 'The Human Motivational Complex: Evolutionary Theory and the Causes of Hunter-Gatherer Fighting, Part I and II, and Debate with Brian Ferguson', *Anthropological Quarterly* (2000), 73:1 (2000), pp. 20–34; 73:2 (2000), pp. 74–88; 73:3, pp. 165–168; idem, 'So Why Do People Fight? Evolutionary Theory and the Causes of War', *European Journal of International Relations*, 15 (2009), pp. 571–599; incorporated into my 2017 book.

5. B. H. Liddell Hart, *Strategy: The Indirect Approach* (London: Faber & Faber, 1967), pp. 211–212, and chapter xxi, 'National Object and Military Aim', pp. 338–352; the book went through several, ever-larger editions, with an evolving title, since its earliest version in 1929. For my study of Liddell Hart, see Azar Gat, *Fascist and Liberal Visions of War: Fuller, Liddell Hart, Douhet and Other Modernists* (Oxford: Clarendon Press, 1998), incorporated into my *History of Military Thought*. See also my *British Armour Theory and the Rise of the Panzer Arm* (London: Macmillan Press, 2000).

6. See Robert Mandel, *The Meaning of Military Victory* (Boulder, CO: Lynne Rienner Publishers, 2006); also, William Martel, *Victory in War: Foundations of Modern Military Policy* (Cambridge: Cambridge University Press, 2007).

7. Edward Luttwak, *Strategy: The Logic of War and Peace* (Cambridge MA: Harvard University Press, 1986).

8. *On War*, III, 1, p. 177; also, II, 1, p. 128. Wherever I deviate from this English translation, the German original is provided within square brackets.

9. Liddell Hart, *Strategy*, pp. 319, 324.

10. *On War*, III, 9, p. 198.

11. Ibid., 10, p. 202.

12. *On War*, IV, 3, pp. 228–229.

13. Ibid., 2, p. 226.

14. Liddell Hart, *Strategy*, 335.
15. Machiavelli, *The Prince*, chapter 18.
16. See notes 11–12, of the Introduction above.
17. Liddell Hart, *Strategy*, 333. Liddell Hart borrowed this idea unacknowledged from the naval theorist Julian Corbett's *Some Principles of Maritime Strategy* (London: Longmans, Green, and Co., 1911); see my 'The Hidden Sources of Liddell Hart's Strategic Ideas', *War in History*, 3, 1996, pp. 293–308. For both Corbett and Liddell Hart, see separately the second and third books of my *History of Military Thought*.
18. *On War*, VI, 1, 2, p. 358.
19. Clausewitz, *Strategie* (1804), section 13.
20. *On War*, VI, 1, 2, p. 358.
21. Ibid., p. 359.
22. Ibid.
23. Raymond Aron, *Clausewitz, den Krieg denken* (Frankfurt am Main: Propyläen Verlag, 1980), pp. 229, 244, and 248–9.
24. *On War*, VI, p. 28.
25. *On War*, I, 2, p. 94.
26. *On War*, VI, p. 26; Gat, *The Clausewitz Myth*, chapter 7.
27. *On War*, VI, 30, p. 502; I, 2, p. 94.
28. Ibid., 1, 2, p. 357; for an almost identical formulation, see ibid., 30, p. 502.
29. Gat, *The Clausewitz Myth*, chapter 7.
30. *On War*, VI, 1, 2, p. 358.
31. Ibid., 3, p. 365.
32. Ibid., 1, 2, p. 358.
33. Works on this theme are a legion. The seminal conceptualization is Robert Jervis, 'Cooperation Under the Security Dilemma', *World Politics*, 30:2 (1978), pp. 167–214. I am not sure, though, about the often far-reaching conclusions drawn in international relations theory from the offense-defense balance, which are indeed in dispute within the discipline itself.
34. For a fuller elaboration, see my *Ideological Fixation: From the*

Stone Age to Today's Culture Wars (Oxford: Oxford University Press, 2022), chapter 1.

2. HISTORY AND MILITARY DOCTRINE

1. See n. 1 of the Introduction, above.
2. *G.S. Isserson and the War of the Future*, translated and edited by Richard Harrison Jefferson (NC: McFarland, 2016 [1932]), Part I.
3. For the debate and my own critique, see my *War in Human Civilization*, pp. 364–365 and n. 80.
4. These ideas repeatedly occur in J. F. C. Fuller's voluminous writings; but see especially his *On Future Warfare* (London: Sifton Praed, 1928); idem, *Armament and History* (London: Charles Scribner's Sons, 1946).
5. Of the many references to these developments, Dennis Showalter, *Rifles and Railroads: Soldiers, Technology and the Unification of Germany* (Hamden, CT: Oxford University Press, 1975) and Daniel Headrick, *The Tools of Empire: Technology and European Imperialism in the Nineteenth Century* (New York: Oxford University Press, 1981) are the most expert.
6. The subject of mechanized land warfare, especially the German, is shrouded in myth. See my *British Armour Theory and the Rise of the Panzer Arm: Revising the Revisionists*, which is based on the documents. More or less similar ground is covered by Mary Habeck, *Storm of Steel: The Development of Armor Doctrine in Germany and the Soviet Union* (Ithaca: Cornell University Press, 2003), which is also the only comprehensive documentary study of Soviet evolution. More generally, see my *Fascist and Liberal Visions of War: Fuller, Liddell Hart, Douhet and Other Modernists*, incorporated into my *A History of Military Thought*. Also, see my 'Ideology, National Policy, Technology and Strategic Doctrine Between

the World Wars', *The Journal of Strategic Studies*, 24:3 (2001), pp. 1–18.

7. Douhet's signature, post-World War I, work is *The Command of the Air* (London: Faber & Faber, 1943; Italian original, 1921). For background and analysis, see my *Fascist and Liberal Visions of War: Fuller, Liddell Hart, Douhet and Other Modernists*, incorporated into my *A History of Military Thought*, pp. 561–597.

8. J. F. C. Fuller, *Towards Armageddon* (London: Lovat Dickson, 1937), pp. 92, 132.

9. James Ray and Ayse Vural, 'Power Disparities and Paradoxical Conflict Outcomes', *International Interactions*, 12 (1986), pp. 315–342.

10. Glenn Snyder, 'Crisis Bargaining', in C. Hermann (ed.), *International Crises: Insights from Behavioral Research* (New York: Free Press, 1972), pp. 232; Steven Rosen, 'War Power and the Willingness to Suffer', in B. Russett (ed.), *Peace, War, and Numbers* (Beverly Hills: Sage Publications, 1972), pp. 167–83; Andrew Mack, 'Why Big Nations Lose Small Wars: The Politics of Asymmetrical Conflict', *World Politics*, 27 (1975), pp. 175–200.

11. Gil Merom, *How Democracies Lose Small Wars: State, Society, and the Failure of France in Algeria, Israel in Lebanon, and the United States in Vietnam* (Cambridge: Cambridge University Press, 2003). While presenting a well-crafted argument about strategic interaction, Ivan Arreguin-Toft, *How the Weak Win Wars: A Theory of Asymmetrical Conflict* (Cambridge: Cambridge University Press, 2005), in effect ends up corroborating Merom's thesis. What he terms a strategy of 'barbarism' turns out in his analysis to be the chief method of suppressing counterinsurgency.

12. For revisionist reappraisals of the alleged critical role of television in Vietnam see: Daniel Hallin, *The "Uncensored War": The Media and Vietnam* (Berkeley: University of

California Press, 1986); William Hammond, *Reporting Vietnam: Media and Military at War* (Lawrence, KS: University Press of Kansas, 1998).

13. Dan Reiter and Allan Stam, *Democracies at War* (Princeton: Princeton University Press, 2002), chapter 7.
14. Alexander Downes, *Targeting Civilians in War* (Ithaca: Cornell University Press, 2008), makes no comparison between democracies and non-democracies in the numbers killed, fails to account for changes in the democracies' behavior during the twentieth century, and does not account the guerrilla wars deterred or cut short by non-democracies' threat of mass killings.
15. David Edelstein, *Occupational Hazards: Success and Failure in Military Occupation* (Ithaca: Cornell University Press, 2008) is an example of this common blind spot for the role of democracy.
16. J. Moor and H. Wesseling (eds.), *Imperialism and War: Essays in Colonial Wars in Asia and Africa* (Leiden: Brill, 1989), pp. 87–120, 121–45, 146–67.
17. Jon Bridgman, *The Revolt of the Hereros* (Berkeley: University of California Press, 1981); Horst Drechsler, *"Let Us Die Fighting": The Struggle of the Herero and Nama against German Imperialism, 1884–1915* (London: Zed Press, 1980); John Iliffe, *Tanganyika under German Rule 1905–1912* (Cambridge: Cambridge University Press, 1969), pp. 9–29; and G. Gwassa and J. Iliffe (eds.), *Record of the Maji Maji Rising* (Nairobi: East African Publishing House, 1967).
18. H. Jack (ed.), *The Gandhi Reader* (Bloomington, Indiana: Indiana University Press, 1956), pp. 317–22, 332–39, 344–47.
19. See, for example, Walter Laqueur's otherwise excellent *The New Terrorism: Fanaticism and the Arms of Mass Destruction* (New York: Oxford University Press, 1999), pp. 8–12.
20. For very early warnings regarding the new potential, see for

example: Philip Cohen, 'A Terrifying Power', *New Scientist* (January 30, 1999), p. 10; Rachel Nowak, 'Disaster in the Making', ibid., (January 13, 2001), pp. 4–5; Carina Dennis, 'The Bugs of War', *Nature* (May 17, 2001), pp. 232–235. I highlighted the threat of biological terrorism in my 2006 and 2017 books, long before the coronavirus pandemic.

21. John Mueller, *Overblown: How Politicians and the Terrorism Industry Inflate National Security Threats and Why We Believe Them* (New York: Free Press, 2006) is a provocative corrective to this threat perception, emphasizing the difficulties of generating unconventional terror, the small number of casualties so far, compared to other sources of mortality, and the counter-effectiveness of many of the measures employed. But it is spoiled by the author's one-sided depreciation of the threat—most notably that of biological weapons—and by his bizarre suggestions that the United States' involvement in World War II and the Cold War were equally unnecessary.

22. See, e.g., Scott Sagan (against) and Kenneth Waltz (for), *The Spread of Nuclear Weapons* (New York: W.W. Norton, 1999); references to terrorist nuclear threat have been added in the second edition (2003), pp. 126–30, 159–66. Also, for, Martin van Creveld, *Nuclear Proliferation and the Future of Conflict* (New York: Free Press, 1993); and a good balanced treatment by Devin Hagerly, *The Consequences of Nuclear Proliferation* (Cambridge, MA: MIT Press, 1998).

23. Graham Allison, *Nuclear Terrorism: The Ultimate Preventable Catastrophe* (New York: Times Books, 2004), is a proposed blueprint for a counter-strategy. It is restricted to the nuclear threat and is not always coherent or persuasive with respect to the available policy options toward proliferation in defiant and weak states.

pp. [104]　　　　　　　　　　NOTES

3.　WAR—NOW AND FOREVER

1. Thomas Hobbes, *The Leviathan* (1651); Jean-Jacques Rousseau, *Discourse on the Origins and Foundation of Inequality among Mankind* (1755).
2. For the refutation of the pacific view of the prehistoric past, see Lawrence Keeley, *War before Civilization* (Oxford: Oxford University Press, 1996); Azar Gat, 'The Pattern of Fighting in Simple, Small Scale, Pre-state Societies', *Journal of Anthropological Research*, 55 (1999), pp. 563–583, and my other works cited in n. 3 of the Introduction, above; Steven LeBlanc, with Katherine Register, *Constant Battles: The Myth of the Peaceful Noble Savage* (New York: St. Martin's Press, 2003); J. Guilaine and J. Zammit, *The Origins of War: Violence in Prehistory* (Malden, MA: Blackwell, 2005) ; R. Wrangham, M. Wilson, and M. Muller, 'Comparative Rates of Violence in Chimpanzees and Humans', *Primates*, 47 (2006), pp. 14–26. Steven Pinker, *The Better Angels of Our Nature: Why Violence Has Declined* (New York: Viking, 2011) has drawn wide public attention to these finds. My last two works on the subject (2015, 2017, see n. 3 of the Introduction, above) demonstrate that there in no basis in reality to the last-ditch attempts to defend Rousseauism by Douglas Fry (ed.), *The Human Potential for Peace* (Oxford: Oxford University Press, 2006), Fry, *War, Peace, and Human Nature: The Convergence of Evolutionary and Cultural Views* (Oxford: Oxford University Press, 2013), and Fry and Patrik Söderberg, 'Lethal Aggression in Mobile Forager Bands and Implications for the Origins of War', *Science*, 341 (2013), pp. 270–273.
3. Sigmund Freud, 'Beyond the Pleasure Principle' (1920); 'The Ego and the Id' (1923); 'Civilization and Its Discontents' (1930); 'New Introductory Lectures on Psychoanalysis' (1933); 'Why War' (1933). All reprinted in *The Complete Psychological Works of Sigmund Freud*, vol. 18, pp. 7–64; vol. 19, pp. 12–66;

vol. 21, pp. 57–145; vol. 22, pp. 5–182, 203–215; Konrad Lorenz, *On Aggression* (London: Methuen, 1966); Robert Ardrey, *The Territorial Imperative* (New York: Atheneum, 1966); Desmond Morris, *The Naked Ape* (London: Jonathan Cape, 1967).

4. Margaret Mead, 'Warfare Is Only an Invention—Not a Biological Necessity', *Asia*, 40:8 (1940), pp. 402–405.
5. Georg Simmel, *Conflict: The Web of Group Affiliations* (Glencoe, IL: Free Press, 1955).
6. The Seville Statement (Paris: UNESCO, 1986).
7. John Mueller, *Retreat from Doomsday: The Obsolescence of Major War* (New York: Basic Books, 1989); Gat, *War in Human Civilization*; idem, *The Causes of War and the Spread of Peace: But Will War Rebound?*; Pinker, *The Better Angels of Our Nature*; Joshua Goldstein, *Winning the War on War: The Decline of Armed Conflict Worldwide* (New York: Dutton, 2011); Ian Morris, *War: What Is It Good For?* (New York: Farrar, Straus and Giroux, 2014).
8. E.g. Stephen Walt, 'An International Relations Theory Guide to the War in Ukraine: A consideration of which theories have been vindicated—and which have fallen flat', *Foreign Policy* (March 8, 2022).
9. The distinction in this regard between the developed and undeveloped or early developers has been variably suggested by some, but has not received sufficient attention by a scholarly community committed to other theories. See Max Singer and Aaron Wildavsky, *The Real World Order: Zones of Peace, Zones of Turmoil* (Chatham, NJ: Chatham House Publishers, 1993); James Goldgeier and Michael McFaul, 'A Tale of Two Worlds: Core and Periphery in the Post-Cold War Era', *International Organization*, p. 46 (1992), pp. 467–91; Håvard Hegre, 'Development and the Liberal Peace: What Does It Take to Be a Trading State?', *Journal of Peace Research*, 37 (2000), pp. 5–30; Michael Mousseau, Håvard Hegre, and John Oneal, 'How the

Wealth of Nations Conditions the Liberal Peace', *European Journal of International Relations*, 9 (2003), pp. 277–314; B. Lacina and N. P. Gleditsch, 'Monitoring Trends in Global Combat: A New Dataset of Battle Deaths', *European Journal of Population*, 21 (2005), pp. 145–166; Azar Gat, 'The Democratic Peace Reframed: The Impact of Modernity', *World Politics*, 58:1 (2005), pp. 73–100, and my 2006 and 2017 books.

10. Arie Kacowicz, *Zones of Peace: South America and West Africa in Comparative Perspective* (New York: State University of New York Press, 1998).

11. John Gaddis, *The Long Peace: Inquiries Into the History of the Cold War* (Oxford: Oxford University Press, 1989).

12. The widely used Correlates of War (COW) database, covering all wars since 1816, has concealed the Long Peace phenomenon from researchers, who are not aware that realities *before* 1816 tell a very different story. But see: Pitirim Sorokin, *Social and Cultural Dynamics*, vol. 3, *Fluctuation of Social Relationships, War, and Revolution* (New York: Bedminster Press, 1962 [1937]); Quincy Wright, *A Study of War* (Chicago: University of Chicago Press, 1965); Jack Levy, *War in the Modern Great Power System, 1495–1975* (Louisville, KT: University Press of Kentucky, 1983); Evan Luard, *War in International Society* (London: I.B. Tauris, 1986); Kalevi Holsti, *Peace and War: Armed Conflicts and International Order 1648–1989* (Cambridge: Cambridge University Press, 1991).

13. Victor Hanson, *A War Like No Other: How the Athenians and Spartans Fought the Peloponnesian War* (New York: Random House, 2005), pp. 10–11, 79–80, 82, 264, 296.

14. Peter Brunt, *Italian Manpower 225 B.C.–A.D. 14* (Oxford: Oxford University Press, 1971).

15. Frederick Mote, 'Chinese Society under Mongol Rule', in H. Franke and D. Twitchett (eds.), *The Cambridge History of China: Alien Regimes and Border States, 907–1368* (Cambridge: Cambridge University Press, 1994), pp. 618-622.

16. Peter Wilson, *The Thirty Years War: Europe's Tragedy* (Cambridge, MA: Harvard University Press, 2009), pp. 786–88.
17. Richard Bonney (ed.), *Economic Systems and State Finance* (Oxford: Oxford University Press, 1995); idem, *The Rise of the Fiscal State in Europe, c. 1200–1815* (Oxford: Oxford University Press, 1999); Gat, *War in Human Civilization*, pp. 371 (and n. 92), 412, 472–476, 484–490.
18. Auguste Comte, 'Plan of the Scientific Operations Necessary for Reorganizing Society' (1822), and 'Course de Philosophie Positive' (1832–42), in G. Lenzer (ed.), *Auguste Comte and Positivism: The Essential Writings* (Chicago: University of Chicago Press, 1975), pp. 37, 293–297; John Stuart Mill, *Principles of Political Economy* (New York: D. Appleton-Century, 1961), book III, chapter xvii, section 5, p. 582.
19. Richard Rosecrance, *The Rise of the Trading State: Commerce and Conquest in the Modern World* (New York: Basic Books, 1986).
20. Mill, *loc. cit.*; Norman Angell, *The Great Illusion* (London: William Heinemann, 1909); John Maynard Keynes, *The Economic Consequences of the Peace* (London: Macmillan, 1919).
21. See my *Nations: The Long History and Deep Roots of Political Ethnicity and Nationalism* (Cambridge: Cambridge University Press, 2013).
22. See Lance Davis and Robert Huttenback, *Mammon and the Pursuit of Empire: The Political Economy of British Imperialism, 1860–1912* (Cambridge: Cambridge University Press, 1986); Dale Copeland, 'Economic Interdependence and War: A Theory of Trade Expectations', *International Security*, 20:4 (1996), pp. 5–41; Gat, *War in Human Civilization*, pp. 554–57, 585.
23. John Mearsheimer, 'Back to the Future: Instability in Europe

after the Cold War', *International Security* 15:1 (1990), pp. 5–56.
24. Azar Gat, 'The Return of Authoritarian Great Powers', *Foreign Affairs* (July–August 2007). For the ensuing debate, see 'Which Way Is History Marching: Debating the Authoritarian Revival', *Foreign Affairs* (July–August 2009).
25. Adam Smith, *The Wealth of Nations*, IV.ii.23.

CONCLUSION

1. For the case for a more historical approach in economics, see recently: Thomas Piketty, *Capital in the Twenty-First Century* (Cambridge MA: Harvard University Press, 2014).
2. Louis Coolidge, *Ulysses S. Grant* (Boston: Houghton Mifflin, 1922), p. 54.

INDEX

Note: Page numbers followed by "*f*" refer to figures.

active defense systems, 64–6
Aelian, 2
Afghanistan, 68, 72, 78, 80, 83, 127
Africa, 77
  imperialism, 125
air warfare, 56, 61–3
al-Assad, Hafez, 81
Aleppo, 82
Algeria, 71, 72, 73
al-Qaeda, 17, 83
American Civil War, 6
Angell, Norman, 121
Aristotle, 134
Armenian army, 64
Aron, Raymond, 36
Arrian, 2
Art of War, The (Machiavelli), 2–3
Art of War, The (Sun Tzu), 134
artillery, 3, 57, 59, 80, 81
Athens, 117–18
Auftragstaktik, 58
Aum Shinrikyo cult (Japan), 93
Australia, 112
Austria, 114, 116
authoritarian regimes, 76–8, 81–2, 87
automation, 62, 66
Azerbaijan, 64

Baader-Meinhof, 88
Baghdad, 25
Belgium, 111
Better Angels of Our Nature, The (Pinker), 108
big data, 62
biological weapons, 91–2
Bloch, Jan, 58
Boer War, 70
Bonaparte, Napoleon, 4–6, 10–12, 19, 30, 34, 36, 39, 141
Britain, 21, 22, 70–1, 79
  imperialism, 125
Buddhism, 108
Bush, George H. W., 25
Byzantine, 2

INDEX

Caesar, Julius 2, 135
Canada, 111
Carthage, 40, 41
Chechnya, 78, 81
chemical warfare, 59, 89–90, 93
China, 12, 20, 22–3, 27, 110, 118, 128–9, 130
   Tibetan insurgency against, 82
Christianity, 108
Churchill, Winston, 8, 23
civil wars, 112
'classics', notion of, 133–4, 135
Clausewitz, Carl von, 9–14, 17–20, 24, 35–9, 45–6, 55, 134, 137
   adversarial and violent, war as, 28–34
   defense and attack relationship, 138
   'historicism', 49–50
Clemenceau, Georges, 21
Cold War, 72, 97–8, 127
colonial wars, 116
computers, 61–2, 140
Comte, Auguste, 121
Corbett, Julian, 7, 33, 135
Counter Enlightenment, 9
cyber terrorism, 94–5
cyber, 62, 66, 140

de Gaulle, Charles, 60
'deep battle', 52

defense and attack relationship, 138
'defense policy', 53
deterrence, 90, 94, 95, 97, 99–100
doctrine, concept of, 50, 54–66, 139, 140
Douhet, Giulio, 61, 135

'East Asian Co-Prosperity Sphere', 77, 126
economic crisis (2007–2008), 129
economic openness, 122, 123
economic theory, 135–7
Egypt, 26
Eisenhower, Dwight D., 22
electronic revolution, 61–3, 140
Enlightenment, 49, 55, 133, 139
Essay on the Principle of Population (Malthus), 120–1
ethnic and nationalist tensions, 124–5
Europe, 9, 12, 23, 61, 79

fascism, 126
Ferdinand, Franz (assassination of), 85
fighting vehicles, 64, 65–6
firearms, 55, 57, 59
France, 7, 21, 71, 72, 73, 119, 125, 126

INDEX

Franco-Prussian War (1870–1871), 20–1
Frederick the Great, 142
Freud, Sigmund, 104
Friedman, Milton, 135
Frontinus, 2
Fuller, J. F. C., 8, 56–7, 60, 62, 135
Future War (Bloch), 58

Gandhi, Mahatma, 79
Gaza, 74–5, 82
GDP per capita, 110, 120*f*
George, David Lloyd, 21
German East Africa (Tanzania), 77
German Southwest Africa (Namibia), 77
Germany, 8, 9, 21, 23, 72, 76, 79, 93, 122, 125, 126, 127
    British starvation blockade of, 73
    non-combatants, killing of, 118–19
    vs. Prussia, 117
    Thirty Years War, casualties, 118
Grand Strategy of the Roman Empire, The (Luttwak), 53
'grand strategy', 53
Grant, Ulysses S., 142
Great Depression, 126
Greece, 2, 12, 122
Grozny, 81

Guderian, Heinz, 60
guerrilla warfare, 67–84
    against the colonial powers, 76–7
    liberal democracies' conduct against, 70–4
    success of, 67, 68, 83–4
    urban environment, insurgents use of, 80–1
Guibert, Comte de, 4–6, 135
Gulf War (1990–1991), 24–5
Gulf War II, 25

Hama (Syria), 81
Hamas, 17
    October 7th 2023 surprise attack, 74–5
Hannibal, 41
Hayek, Friedrich, 135
Herero revolt (1904), 77
Hezbollah, 17
high-tech warfare, 83
Hindenburg, Paul von 21
Hobbes, Thomas, 44, 103–4, 109
Holland, 111
Holmes, Sherlock, 76, 77–8
Hungary, 78
Hussein, Saddam, 25

Iberian Peninsula, 34
imperial 'pacification', 69–70
imperialism, 125, 126
India, 12, 20, 79, 97

INDEX

Industrial Revolution, First, 50, 54–5, 57, 58, 119–21
Industrial Revolution, Second, 56, 59–61, 140
Industrial-Technological or Information Revolution, Third, 61–3
Influence of Sea Power upon History, 1660–1783, The (Mahan), 7
International Atomic Energy Agency (IAEA), 99
Iran, 91, 98, 99
Iraq, 24–5
Ireland, 70–1, 73
irregular warfare. *See* guerrilla warfare terrorism
ISIS, 17, 83
Israel/Israelis, 20, 26, 73–5, 83
    Hamas' October 7th 2023 surprise attack, 74–5
Israeli Air Force, 81
Israeli Trophy system, 64
Isserson, Georgi, 52
Italy, 41, 123

Japan, 72, 76-77, 112, 126
Jihadist terrorism, 88, 89
Jomini, Antoine-Henri, 6–7, 8–9, 135
Just and Unjust Wars (Walzer), 75

Kautilya, 12

Kennedy, John F., 99
Keynes, John Maynard, 121–2, 135
Khan, Abdul Qadeer, 91
Kissinger, Henry, 26
Korea, 77
Korean War, 22
Kuwait, 24–5

land warfare, mechanization of 56, 58-60,
Lebanon, 82, 83
Leo (Byzantine emperor), 2
'levels', of the conduct of war, 51–3
liberal democracies, 69–74, 80, 112, 123–4, 127
Libya, 91
Liddell Hart, Basil, 24, 30–1, 33, 60, 135
Lincoln, Abraham, 108
Long Peace, 114–17, 115*f*, 119, 124
Ludendorff, Eric, 21
Luttwak, Edward, 29, 53

MacArthur, Douglas, 22–3, 138
Machiavelli, Niccolò, 2–4, 7, 34, 54, 135
Mahan, Alfred, 6–8, 61, 135
Maji–Maji revolt (1905–1907), 77
Malthus, Thomas, Malthusian Trap, 120–2

INDEX

Manchuria, 77
Mao Zedong, 27
Maurice (Byzantine emperor), 2
Mead, Margaret, 105
Merom, Gil, 69
Mill, John Stuart, 119, 121
Moltke, Helmut von, 20–1
Mongol conquests, 118
mutual assured destruction (MAD), 97–8, 100, 101

Napoleon, *see* Bonaparte
nationalism, 125
naval warfare, 56, 57–8, 61, 62–3
Nazism, Nazi Germany, 76, 78, 84
Nelson, Horatio, 7–8
New Zealand, 112
9/11 terror attack, 85, 93, 94
non-violent resistance, 79
North Africa, 41, 111
North Korea, 91, 97, 110
Nuclear Non-Proliferation Treaty (NPT), 99
nuclear weapons, 90–2, 95–101, 126

On War (Clausewitz), 11–13, 24, 49
'operations, 'operational art', 'operational level', 52, 53, 58

Pakistan, 91, 97
Palestinian Authority, 83
Palestinian Intifadas, 74
Peloponnesian War (431–403 BCE), 117–18
Pinker, Steven, 108
Plato, 134
Poland, 78
Polanyi, Karl, 135
Polyaen, 2
Polybius, 2
Prince, The (Machiavelli), 34
'principles of war', 56, 139, 140–1, 143
protectionism, 125, 130
Prussia, 10, 19, 114, 116
Punic War, Second (218–216 BCE), 40, 118
Putin, Vladimir, 78–9
'Pyrrhic victory', 24

'realists' in international relations theory, 110, 112, 127
Red Army, 88
Red Brigades, 88
'Revolution in Military Affairs', term, 63
revolutions in warfare, 54–66, 139–40
Ricardo, David, 135
Romantic Movement, 9
Rome, ancient, 40, 41, 118
Roosevelt, Franklin D., 22

INDEX

Rossbach, Battle of, 142
Rousseau, Jean-Jacques, 103–4
Russia, 129–130. *See also* Soviet Union
   counterinsurgency campaigns, 81–2
Russia–Ukraine War, 62, 64, 81, 109, 131
   nuclear weapons, 98

Saint-Simon, Henri de, 121
Schelling, Thomas, 16
Seven Years' War, 142
Seville Statement on Violence, 106–7
Seydlitz, Friedrich Wilhelm von, 142
Six-Day War (1967), 26
Smith, Adam, 130, 135
Some Principles of Maritime Strategy (1911) (Corbett), 7–8
South Africa, 70
South China Sea, 110, 130
South Korea, 112
South Lebanese Army, 83
Soviet Union, 23, 60, 68, 72, 76, 78–9, 91, 96–98, 118, 127
Spain, 36, 41, 119
Stalin, Joseph, 78
strategy and tactics, 51–3
Strategy: The Indirect Approach (Liddell Hart), 31

Sun Tzu, 12, 31, 134
Syria, 26
   civil war (2015), 81

Taiwan, 77, 110, 112, 130
tanks, 60, 63–4, 65
technological revolution, fourth wave of, 62
terrorism, 84–95
   biological weapons, 91–2
   chemical weapons, use of, 89–90
   communication technology, and, 86–7, 89
   cyber terrorism, 94–5
   against democracies, 88
   national liberation and social revolution, 88
   normative perspective, 84–5
   nuclear weapons, 90–2, 94
   as a public relations act, 87–8
   success of, 87–8
   against totalitarian/ authoritarian regimes, 87
   weapons of mass destruction (WMD), 89–90, 92
Thirty Years War (1618–1648), 118
Thucydides, 12

INDEX

Tokyo chemical attack (1995), 93
Truman, Harry S., 22–3

Ukraine, 65
   Russian invasion of (2022), 109
   See also Russia–Ukraine War
UNESCO, 106
United Kingdom, 70–1, 73
United Nations, 22–3
United States Military Academy, 142
United States, 8, 24–5, 61, 80, 81, 83, 93, 94, 109, 125, 126
   American hegemony, 127
   nuclear power, 96, 97–8
unmanned aerial vehicles, 65
urban environment, insurgents use of, 80–1
urbanization, 123
US Army, 33

Vegetius, 2, 135
Victory, meaning of, 22–28
Vietnam War, 71
violence and human biology, 103–9
Vitruvius, 2

Walzer, Michael, 75
war, nature of, 10–12, 14, 44
   adversarial and violent, war as, 28–34
   defense and attack, 34–42
   definitions, 42–8
   and politics, 17–28
   and human nature, 103–9
   'wars by proxy', 116–17
Wealth of Nations (Smith), 135
weapons of mass destruction (WMD), 89, 92
web communication, 62
Wellington, Duke of, 34
West Bank, 74, 83
Western Europe, 127–8
'winning the hearts and minds', 80
World War I, 21, 38, 52, 53, 60, 61, 65, 73, 86, 126
World War II, 8, 12–13, 22, 61, 63, 64, 73, 77, 79, 86, 117, 118–19

Xenophon, 2, 135

Yom Kippur War (1973), 26
Yugoslavia, 78

Zhou Enlai, 27
'zone of peace', 110, 111, 112, 113*f*, 114, 131
'zone of war', 110–12, 113*f*, 131